A Commentary on
THE PERSONAL LETTERS

UNLOCKING THE NEW TESTAMENT

A Commentary on
THE PERSONAL LETTERS
1 & 2 Timothy, Titus, Philemon

David Pawson

> This book is a gift
> to your College Library
> from David Pawson
> and the David Pawson Teaching Trust
> Joshua 1:8

Anchor Recordings

Copyright © 2015 David Pawson

The right of David Pawson to be identified as author of this Work has been asserted by him in accordance with the Copyright, Designs and Patents Act 1988.

First published in Great Britain in 2015 by
Anchor Recordings Ltd
72 The Street, Kennington, Ashford TN24 9HS

No part of this publication may be reproduced or transmitted in any form or by any means, electronic or mechanical, including photocopy, recording or any information storage and retrieval system, without prior permission in writing from the publisher.

For more of David Pawson's teaching, including DVDs and CDs, go to www.davidpawson.com

**FOR FREE DOWNLOADS
www.davidpawson.org**

**For further information, email
info@davidpawsonministry.org**

ISBN 978-1-909886-70-4

Printed by Lightning Source

Contents

INTRODUCTION – PASTORAL LETTERS	9
1 TIMOTHY 1	23
1 TIMOTHY 2	41
1 TIMOTHY 3	57
1 TIMOTHY 4	73
1 TIMOTHY 5	87
1 TIMOTHY 6	101
2 TIMOTHY 1:1–2:13	115
2 TIMOTHY 2:14–3:9	131
2 TIMOTHY 3:10–4:22	151
TITUS	167
PHILEMON	217

This book is based on a series of talks. Originating as it does from the spoken word, its style will be found by many readers to be somewhat different from my usual written style. It is hoped that this will not detract from the substance of the biblical teaching found here.

As always, I ask the reader to compare everything I say or write with what is written in the Bible and, if at any point a conflict is found, always to rely upon the clear teaching of scripture.

David Pawson

INTRODUCTION
– PASTORAL LETTERS

1. When?

2. Why?
    a. Credal – orthodoxy
    b. Constitutional – organisation

People have put Paul's letters into several categories. One group has been called the *travel* epistles, meaning those he wrote while he was travelling around – epistles such as 1 and 2 Corinthians, Romans, Galatians and so on. A second group has been called the *prison* epistles – even when Paul was chained to a Roman soldier, he still could not be stopped from writing letters. He wrote to the Philippians from prison, for example. But 1 and 2 Timothy (like Titus) don't fit into either of these categories, they have been treated separately right through church history, and have been given various titles. The first was the *personal* epistles. They were called this because they are addressed not to churches but to an individual, and they are full of deep affection.

In these letters, more than any other, the friendship that Paul had for people comes across, and particularly for the person to whom the letter was addressed. They are conversational; they are chatty letters. They are much more informal than the letter to the Romans, for example, or Ephesians, both of which flow like a mighty river. These are almost like a babbling brook tinkling over the stones, and little thoughts keep rushing out as in conversation.

After the early period, for the next thousand years these little letters were called the *pontifical* letters – a horrible title, but they were called that because they were regarded as the rules for the priesthood of the church. In a very real sense, these letters are directed to ministers, pastors, deacons, elders – those who are responsible for leading the fellowship of Christ. Indeed, here is a good manual on shepherding.

When I was training in agriculture, one of the books I had to study was a manual on shepherding. We had to learn just about everything we could about sheep, learning about so many diseases that I despaired of ever having a healthy sheep in the flock! It told us what to do with their feet when they went wrong, and what to do about many other things. I hope this won't cause you to shudder, but I remember as a young student having to learn to sew eyelids open of little lambs that had been born blind. That was my first practical in shepherding. I had read the book about it, but it is different getting down to doing it. I was enabling sheep to see, and I learned that way. When I became a pastor, people asked "Well, wasn't all that agricultural training wasted?" No, I remained a shepherd. I don't do it quite as drastically now, but a pastor has a job: to help his people to see – to open blind eyes, by the grace of God, so that they can see the truth of God. These letters of Paul are a manual of shepherding: how to look after sheep, what you do with them when they are straying, what you do when they need food, and so on. So these epistles were given to the priests for a thousand years as a manual for looking after sheep and they are still very fine advice for ministry today.

But about the year 1274, a famous Catholic theologian, Thomas Aquinas, coined a new title. He did not like the word "pontifical" which sounds a bit pompous, so he coined a lovely new title – the *pastoral* letters. It was not used for another five hundred years, and then a Frenchman used it again, and since then it has stuck: the "shepherding epistles", the "looking-after-sheep epistles". Here Paul devotes himself to pastoral problems which are not so much problems of basic Christian belief, nor even problems of basic Christian behaviour, but problems of church life – looking after the flock, keeping the people together, keeping the sheep healthy and shepherding them one-by-one. So I am going to stick to the title: the *pastoral letters* of Paul.

Now I want to deal with a problem you may have heard about: who wrote these letters? It says at the top of the page:

INTRODUCTION – PASTORAL LETTERS

"The first letter of Paul to Timothy" and "The second letter of Paul to Timothy", but of course those titles have been added later, and many people have questioned whether Paul was the author. It is important to settle this issue at the outset. I want to be fair and explain why many people today would say that these letters are not from Paul. I believe they are, and I will give my reasons for believing that. Why should anybody question that Paul wrote these letters? Four reasons are: historical, literary, theological, and ecclesiastical. First of all, there is an *historical* problem: piecing together the little hints in these letters as to where Paul was, where his companions were and what was happening to him as the details we get do not fit easily into the sequence in Acts. For example, Paul has visited Crete, which he never did in Acts. He has visited Necropolis, and he was never anywhere near there in Acts. We find Paul in prison at the end of Acts, awaiting execution. Although he had never been to Crete, in these letters he says, "I've been to Crete"; "when I was there...." It is that kind of problem. The friends of Paul who are mentioned in these letters seem to have got to the wrong place. Timothy is now in Ephesus, whereas really he was left in Asia. Demas has deserted from Rome; in Acts he was somewhere else. Mark is in Asia, Tychicus is in Ephesus, and Luke is with Paul in Rome in prison. If you study the narrative in Acts carefully, not one of those people is now where they should be. Of course, some people jump up and shout, "There you are, contradictions in the Bible again!" Well, we will look at that a little more carefully.

The second difficulty some have with these letters is a *literary* one. The style of the pastoral letters is quite different from the style of Paul's other letters. Have you ever had a letter from someone and thought: "Is that really from them? It reads so differently; it's just not like them to write like this." Many have felt that way. For example, Paul uses in these letters just over nine hundred different words, and over one-third of those words he never uses in any other letters. They appear all through these letters but are never used in Romans, Corinthians, Galatians or Ephesians. It was on this basis that a computer analysis was said to indicate that Paul did not write them. But computers can only give out what you feed in. The computer had been told that if there are any words that are different then the letter could not come from the same person. So we must not blame the computer for what was said, but the scholar who inputted the criteria. If it were true that a person cannot change their vocabulary and cannot use new words, then of course these letters would not be from Paul. But the difficulty is that he uses so many different ones. Furthermore, there are some words which are never used in these letters that are used in others. For example the word "cross" never occurs – nor even the word "crucify". The words "freedom", "liberty" and "slavery" never occur. The words "son" and "adoption", favourite words of Paul, are absent.

Furthermore, when Paul really gets going in most of his letters, he writes sentences that do not seem to stop! One in Ephesians is fourteen verses long, and if you pause and analyse it, there is not even a main verb. It looks as if he just stopped and said: better start another sentence. He flows – one clause after another. But that never happens in these letters. There are no long sentences, just short, chatty phrases one after the other, like machine gun fire instead of the big guns.

The third kind of difficulty people have had is *theological*. The ideas seem to be rather different. I will give you the most outstanding example straight away. One of Paul's great ideas is *faith* – to believe in Jesus. The apostle talks about faith and walking by faith, but in these letters, instead of talking about the faith as a personal relationship to Jesus, he talks about '*the* faith' as a written creed, as a form of sound words to be recited and passed on. This is a real tension. Is faith a relationship to a person or a creed in words? Certainly, in the earlier letters of Paul he emphasises the relationship to a person – faith is what I have towards Jesus. But here he emphasises faith as a creed, which is to be recited and passed on in the exact form of words from one generation to the next, and that is a big change. Another example is that the Holy Spirit is only mentioned rarely in the pastoral epistles, which is pretty remarkable for Paul and contrasts with the earlier letters.

The fourth difficulty some people have with these letters is that there is a situation in the churches referred to which is very different from that reflected in Acts. They now have bishops – not the kind of bishops we know today, who look after a wide area, but definitely people called bishops, elders or overseers. There now seems to be an established order of bishops.

More than that, there is also the matter of paid teachers and this again is a remarkable change. So much so that some Christian bodies to this day deny the rightness of having paid teaching elders, but in 1 Timothy there they are. The elders of the church who labour in preaching and teaching are paid. As far as we know, that did not happen in the time of Acts – at least it is not specifically mentioned. This is a new kind of pattern. There is also an order of widows. Widows were enrolled into a kind of community of sisters in the church. That was not there before.

So here are four problems: historical, literary, theological and envisaging a kind of church organisation that did not exist before. What is the answer? Some scholars say it is that Paul cannot be the author. Even if he wrote a few little bits, somebody else has been rewriting or editing it, and in fact it is a compilation at a much later date by editors who were trying to make Paul say something that they approved of. So they wrote their ideas of bishops and all the rest into Paul's letters and then circulated them under Paul's name so everybody would accept them. That is the most commonly accepted view of these letters which has been taught in theological colleges.

I want to put to you another alternative explanation which to me covers most if not all of these difficulties. It begins by asking two simple questions: *when* and *why* were these letters written? Let us go back to the last chapter in Acts. Paul is in prison in Rome and the book of Acts finishes. The occasion when he lost his head to a Roman executioner's sword is not mentioned. Furthermore, in Acts and other letters there is clear indication that Paul believed in Roman justice enough to be looking forward to being released. He expected to be able to go on further missionary journeys, and he wanted to go to Spain. His ambition was to cover the whole Mediterranean world. He had evangelised the eastern half of the Mediterranean right to Italy. I can understand that he would have wanted to go further. Jesus had said, "Go into all the world...."

At least four ancient documents have been discovered which tell us that Paul was released and re-captured some years later, and then executed – that in fact there was (though not recorded in the Bible) a further missionary tour which Paul later undertook. Having been released by Roman justice from the trial mentioned at the end of Acts, he went on his travels again and carried on preaching. Then later, when the persecution under Nero stepped up again, he was arrested and unjustly executed as many others were in those days. I am not going to give you all the details of that. His hopes for release you can find in Philippians chapters two and four. The traditions I have mentioned which suggest that he did have a further missionary tour come from writings like those of Eusebius, Clement, Chrysostom and Jerome—two of whom say he got as far as Spain before he was finally re-arrested and put back on trial.

Here is perhaps one of the most thrilling unwritten stories of church history, a whole chapter that never got put in Acts. If that happened, then everything mentioned in the pastoral letters would dovetail into an ordered pattern, and the problem simply disappears.

That settles one problem but not the others. It does mean, however, that these letters are the very latest that Paul wrote, and that where in 2 Timothy he describes that he feels he is going to be put on trial and will not escape, this is now his second imprisonment in Rome, and this time he knows that Nero the emperor will have no sympathy at all. So he says, "The time of my departure is at hand. I'm waiting for the crown of life," and his death is there. So here you have Paul's last words and here you have his very last letters as an older, more experienced man. But that still does not cover all the problems. Yet if what I have written about the timescale is correct, and if we ask why he wrote these letters, the answer comes through loud and clear. He wrote the pastoral letters for a very different purpose from the reasons for which he wrote Romans, Corinthians, Galatians, Ephesians and so on. If what I have indicated about the "when" is right, the answer to the "why" is this: he is now coping with churches in the second and third generation of Christians. When you are in that situation, what you say is completely different from what you say to a church that has just started. By and large, churches go through two stages in their history—stage number one: the stage of evangelising. There is no church there. Somebody comes and starts preaching in the open air or a borrowed room, anywhere that people will come, and the church begins to form, people begin to be saved. The message then is: faith is belief in Christ. Paul was normally involved in stage number one: starting churches. He was an evangelist to them. But when you are dealing with churches that are second and third generation, then what you need is a pastor to edify rather than an evangelist to evangelise. The second stage in the life of a church is also concerned with pastoral problems. Today, an evangelist can come for some days and preach the gospel, then people are converted, they believe in Jesus and new life starts. That is one problem over. But, from another point of view, other problems have just begun. The other problems that have begun are to do with the pastoral care of the people. One of the things they now need is this: they have faith in Jesus, it is now necessary to teach them *the* faith in the form of sound words so that they have a grasp of what they believe and how they are to behave. For example, someone may come to Christ and be converted without knowing that Jesus is coming back to earth. They need to be taught that is part of the faith that Jesus is coming back again. Therefore, once a person has faith, the emphasis then must be on *the* faith – the Christian creed, the form of sound words; what we believe and how we express it for others.

You can see, therefore, that once a person has been evangelised and is now in this situation, you need to change what you say to them – not because the first stage was wrong but because they are past that. They have now gone beyond the elementary things, the milk stage, and they need the meat. They need to feed and grow. Now if Paul is writing not to people who are being evangelised but to the leaders of the church, is it not understandable that he should change even his manner of writing? If you deal with different subjects, you tackle them in different ways. Sometimes I write a chatty letter to someone, dealing with a few little points. Somebody else has asked a question about what I think about the millennium – who can answer that with a short, chatty

INTRODUCTION – PASTORAL LETTERS

letter? Usually it extends into quite a paper and becomes rather ponderous and heavy. You change your style; you even change your language when you are sending a different kind of letter. This explains to me what has happened. Paul is writing to churches that are built up and established, and there are two things a church like that needs. You don't need them in evangelism. You don't need them with conversion. But you need them with churches of the second and third generation. The two greatest needs of an established church, if it is going to go on in a powerful way, are *orthodoxy* and *organisation*. If those two things are not right, and if a church slips in its orthodoxy or gets haphazard in its organisation, then the church will not continue. Tragically, some people naively think that what enables you to start the Christian life is all you need thereafter. They say, "What do we need with creeds, and what do we need with church meetings and organisation? Let's just all get filled with the Spirit as we were at our conversion, and the place will really be on fire." That's the devil's half-truth. Of course we need the Holy Spirit; of course we need the zeal of the Lord – but we need to look at our orthodoxy and our organisation. This is the framework within which the Holy Spirit works in a continuing work that is going to last for many years.

One of Paul's major concerns through the pastoral letters is that the churches which Timothy is looking after as pastor should have an adequate confession of faith, that they should have a detailed form of sound words which they all believe, so that anybody joining the church can be told, "This is what we believe; this is where we stand; this is the truth as we understand it." So he pleads with Timothy to get a good confession of faith that can be passed on to succeeding generations so that there may be no doubt what the church believes.

There is an interesting big book called *Baptists'*

Confessions of Faith. It really does deal with those who say that Baptists don't believe in creeds. Don't they? They have far more than Anglicans – pages of them, marvellous statements of faith, wonderful confessions of what is believed and why. It is thrilling to read and you can understand why Baptists did become the largest Protestant group in the world. They knew where they stood; they knew what they believed. This was their strength and they knew that if a church gets away from orthodoxy, if it gets away from what is really the faith of the apostles, you must expect that church's days to be numbered. I admit this with some embarrassment, but the only group of Baptists who got away from that were the British ones, and numerical decline followed.

One of the concerns of a church that has been established for a long time is that it should only pass on the one true faith, contending for the faith once delivered to the saints. Christianity has not changed, and it never will. It is our solemn responsibility to pass it on to the next generation.

The other thing a church needs is *organisation*. There are those who belittle organisation compared with spiritual fervour but let me give you a parable. When you first strike oil – what happens? It comes gushing up and it hits the air, and sometimes it catches fire spontaneously. It burns, and you can see the fire for miles—tremendous, they know they have hit power and there it is blazing away. If you go back to that same spot ten years later, you will not see such fireworks. You will see a flame burning off waste gases, but you will also see pipes, machinery and refineries. What has been done? People will say, "It's not as interesting to look at, not nearly as spectacular." No, it isn't, but organisation has channelled the power to where it is needed. The fire is still there, but now it has been piped to where it ought to burn to help people. Therefore, when you are in a new situation, a pioneer situation with no church – when you are blazing

INTRODUCTION – PASTORAL LETTERS

away, and evangelising here, there and everywhere – it is wonderful, spectacular. You go to some churches and it looks so ordered. Mind you, it can be the order of a cemetery, but even so, if it's not, if the members are alive, it is still ordered. Let not people misunderstand—the organisation of the church, with its membership rule, its church meeting and its leaders, is seeking to channel the fire to people who need it. Otherwise things might be too haphazard.

That is why the letters to Timothy are concerned with elders and deacons – the kind of setup you need in a church that is going to go on caring for people. So you have the organisation developing and Paul is not now writing of the gospel, he is concerned with orthodoxy and organisation, deacons and paid elders, a team in the church who are to lead its affairs. You can see why it was necessary and why he wrote these letters. Therefore I believe that Paul wrote them at a different time and for a different purpose than the others, and that this explains the differences. In any event, the pastoral letters are the word of God to us just as much as the rest of scripture. We take the whole word of God.

Read 1 Timothy 1

From Paul – authority and affection
To Timothy – grace, mercy and peace

A. THE LAW (3–11)
- 1. Its perversion (3–11)
  - a. Imagination
    - i. Myths and endless genealogies
    - ii. Speculations and vain discussions
  - b. Instruction
    - i. Pure heat ii. Good conscience
    - iii. Sincere faith
- 2. Its purpose (8–11)
  - a. Against God
    - i. Irresponsible – lawless and disobedient
    - ii. Irreligious – ungodly and sinning
    - iii. Irreverent – unholy and profane
  - b. Against man
    - i. Murderers (of parents) ii. Manslayers
    - iii. Sodomites
    - iv. Kidnappers (lit. slave dealers)
    - v. Liars (and perjurers)

B. THE GOSPEL (12–20)
- 1. Its purpose (12–17)
  - a. Mercy of the Saviour
    - i. Who? Christ Jesus –
    - ii. What? came into the world –
    - iii. Why? to save sinners
  - b. Majesty of the Sovereign
    - i. Immortal ii. Invisible iii. Incomparable
- 2. Its perversion (18–20)
  - a. Good soldier
    - i. Kept faith ii. Good conscience
  - b. Bad sailor
    - i. Bad conscience ii. Lost faith

Timothy was born in Lystra, a Roman outpost, of a Greek father and a Jewish mother. The religion, as in many families, seems to have been on the female side. His mother, Eunice, and his grandmother, Lois, were godly people. They were both Christian Jews, and there is no Christian like a Christian Jew. Have you ever met one? Don't you sometimes feel, "I wish I had been a Jew, with this unique combination of being part of the people of the Old Testament and the people of the New"?

From when he was a very little boy, Timothy had been taught the scriptures. They did not have the New Testament yet, but the Old Testament is a Christian book too, and his grandmother and mother taught him the Old Testament – his father was probably at business all the time. Timothy was a delicate boy – not very strong, rather timid. Yet God called him to be a pastor through a word of prophecy. I am quite sure that if they had a church meeting, they would have said, "No, Timothy is not the kind to be a pastor – he's not strong, not very forceful, not a leader." But God, through a word of prophecy said, "Ordain Timothy," and Timothy was made a pastor. Paul told him to take a little wine for his stomach trouble. This delicate, timid young man found himself pastoring a number of churches. Paul looked on him as though he were his own son. Paul was not married, but he had a big family and some of them were especially dear to him. Timothy was one of his closest friends. For him he had an affection that he had for few others. This young man was now faced with the awesome responsibility of looking after churches. So Paul takes his pen and writes to him. He is instructing Timothy not to let them look down on him for his youth. Don't let them push you around. Give them the kind of leadership that ought to be given in a second and third generation church. So Paul speaks with authority and affection. That is the perfect combination for pastoral leadership: to speak with authority – let it be known, I have the command of God behind me; and to speak with affection – you are my children, my brothers, my sisters, my family.

The letter begins in the most sensible way: from Paul to Timothy. No beating about the bush. Then Paul gives a greeting with three of the loveliest words in the New Testament: "Grace, mercy and peace...." Could you wish anybody anything more than that? Not health and wealth, good luck to you, — no, it is "grace, mercy, and peace". If you have those, then you can go on to orthodoxy and organisation. If you do not know grace, mercy and peace, then do not go any further. Get those things clear first. Grace is the favour of God that gives us what we don't deserve, that pours out upon us constant gifts, God's riches at Christ's expense "g-r-a-c-e". "Mercy" is to be forgiven for the wrong things we have done. "Peace" means that peace you have inside you when you have a clear conscience, when God has forgiven you your sins and is pouring his grace into your life. That is the foundation. If I mention it only briefly here, don't get me wrong. We dare not discuss anything concerned with what we believe or how we organise until we are quite clear that we are children of grace, mercy and peace from God our Saviour and Christ, our only hope.

Agricultural illustrations seem to drop into place as I read these letters. I well remember one of my worst mornings ever. I still recall the horrible, empty feeling I had that day. I was looking after some calves – I was responsible for them and they belonged to one of the top pedigree herds. When they reached twelve-months old, they would fetch anywhere between a thousand and fifteen hundred pounds. I had about a dozen or fifteen of them in my personal charge. That morning

I came down to feed them and two were lying dead, two more were having convulsions and the others were looking sick. I shall never forget that moment as I saw thousands of pounds just disappearing. All the symptoms were of lead poisoning. I remember searching the cowshed, looking at lead pipes to see if they had been chewing those, and could not find any trace at all. Finally, we had to do a post-mortem on one – more were dying all the time. We found in the stomach of one of the calves some tiny shreds of lead. One of them was larger than the others and we recognised it as an air-gun slug. A few weeks earlier, the farmer had given his son an air gun for his birthday and he had been lying in the Dutch barn where all the corn was stored, shooting sparrows for weeks, filling that corn with little pellets of lead, which had then been ground up with the corn and fed to the calves. They were only tiny pieces, but added to the good corn that I was feeding them, it was deadly. I was profoundly relieved to discover that technically it was not my direct responsibility, though it was still a tragedy and we felt it for a long time. That was my experience in looking after animals. When I became a pastor of people I was given a solemn charge from the scripture to be equally careful about what is fed to the flock. For the task of a pastor, as in the case of Timothy here, is not only to see that the flock get good food, but also to see that they do not get bad food. That is the less popular and less pleasant of the tasks of a pastor today, in an age where we seem to tolerate anyone's opinion about anything. It does not need much to be added to the truth of God to make it poisonous to people. It just needs a little bit of speculation here and a little bit of twisting there, and what you are feeding to people becomes deadly to them and will destroy their spiritual health. Therefore it is the solemn responsibility of a pastor, before God, not only to seek to give good food, but to see that anyone who mixes it with anything dangerous does not teach the flock. The reason is that it is a matter of life and death. In these days it would seem that people think that as long as you are sincere it doesn't matter what you believe and everyone is entitled to their own opinion or interpretation. I remember reading in the newspapers of how some newborn twins needed emergency surgery, and during the operation the surgeon turned to the sister and asked her to hand him a syringe full of a certain drug—quickly. She ran to the cupboard, filled a hypodermic syringe, passed it to the doctor who injected the babies, and they both died. When she looked again at the cupboard, with horror she realised that she had taken something from the wrong bottle. At the inquiry that was held later she said, "I sincerely believed I had taken the right bottle." The chairman of the inquiry said, "I believe that you are sincere, but you were sincerely wrong and you gave the wrong thing." It is as serious as that.

So Paul is saying: I charge you my son Timothy, don't leave Ephesus until you have stopped those false teachers in the church teaching things that are poison; until you have made sure that the congregation is going to go on getting good food – then you can come and join me and we will move on to other churches. You see, Paul was an evangelist, a missionary, and he was bringing spiritual babies into the world. He was concerned that they should get the right milk, and then meat. How would you feel if a baby had died because someone else had not fed it properly? You would feel terrible, and Paul therefore writes to Timothy: as I urged you when I was going to Macedonia, you stay there and charge certain persons not to teach wrong doctrine.

One of the clichés that I have heard so frequently I am getting tired of it is: "Let's keep off doctrine because doctrine divides." Of course doctrine divides! It divides between truth and error – it is as radical as that. There is truth and there is falsehood, and doctrine will always divide. True doctrine unites those who want the truth, but it does not unite anyone else.

Therefore, Paul is concerned in these letters to Timothy with doctrine, teaching, truth, food that will help people to grow and be strong and healthy in the Lord. Now what kind of false teaching was being given? It was teaching derived from scripture, from the law of Moses. The teachers Paul refers to he does not name out of courtesy, but he nevertheless says what they teach. The teachers he refers to were turning Bible study into a purely academic and speculative entertainment, and breeding a church full of intelligence but not full of good Christians. They were taking the law and they were speculating about it and going beyond what the scriptures said, speculating about myths, legends, endless genealogies and other things. We can understand that, because in those days people just loved that kind of thing. If you study Greek religion and read all about the doings of their gods and all the myths and legends about them, you realise they love this kind of rubbish, and even Jews loved it too. There are books that did not get into our Bible – thank God they didn't. The book of Jubilees is one, written by Jews. They are pure speculation, filled with endless genealogies. They were full of things that people wanted to discuss that scripture did not deal with.

It is terribly easy to run off into intellectual academic speculations, which are vain discussion, which the Bible does not deal with. I will give you an example: the origin of evil. The Bible only gives us one or two hints but it does not directly deal with where evil came from. It does deal with where evil is going to, which is the more important thing – because wherever it came from, we know where it is going, and we want to save people from going there. It is intellectual speculation to ask about the origin of evil. It is a mystery that God has seen fit not to declare fully. There are only a few hints that it began among the angels rather than men and spilled over into this world, but it is speculation to ask any more than that. Speculation does not help. It simply leads to an intellectual sharpening of axes as we grind them on each other's grindstone – and that is all it does. No-one was ever saved by telling them of the origin of evil; they were saved by telling them of the destiny of evil.

So the Bible doesn't tell us certain things that we would love to know. Let me give you another example of the kind of speculative addition to scripture that is taking place. Have you ever heard of the Gospel of the Hebrews, or the Gospel of Thomas? You have heard of the Gospels of Matthew, Mark, Luke and John, but there are apocryphal Gospels. In those "Gospels" are legends and myths about our Lord as a boy. I will give you two of them: one is that one day a boy in Nazareth pushed Jesus into a puddle. Jesus stood up and cursed the boy and he was a leper from that day on—that is from the Gospel of the Hebrews. Another legend about Jesus is that one day he took some mud and he made little models of birds and then he blessed them and they turned into real birds and flew away. You can read all that kind of rubbish in the "Gospel" of Thomas. Around the figure of Jesus have gathered many legends, myths and speculation as to what he did as a boy for eighteen years in the carpenter's shop, but the Bible contains none of this. It is pure speculation to read these legends and discuss them, and it will not save you one bit. That story about him making birds and watching them fly away never saved anybody. Which is one reason it isn't in the Bible. The other is that it is not true. There were also legends that the Jews developed about Moses.

The Apocrypha is not the word of God. It is a collection of books written between the period when the prophets gave the word of God, which began with Moses and ended with

Malachi, and the period when the apostles gave the word of God. Both groups of people said, "Thus says the Lord," a phrase that never occurs in the Apocrypha because it is not a collection of books of divine revelation, but of human religion. It is the most dangerous book to have bound up with the word of God. If you want to read the Apocrypha, buy it separately, as a human book, but don't put it in the word of God. It is not the word of God but an addition to the word of God, and it leads to speculation. I will give you an illustration of how it does: in the Apocrypha, they began to get weird ideas about the dead. It is significant that the Apocrypha is so often read at funerals and that disturbs me too. But one of the things taught in the Apocrypha is that it is all right to pray for dead people. That is something the Bible never encourages, indeed the Old Testament forbids. But if you put the Apocrypha into the word of God, you start praying for the dead, a practice that is open to much abuse and superstition and which can do no good anyway.

This is enough to indicate what was happening at Ephesus. Men were speculating, adding to the scriptures, and they were developing a teaching which was not really to be found there. It was purely intellectual – they fancied themselves as scholars, they wanted to be teachers of the law, and they were popular because people love novelty, legends, myths and speculation, anything but the truth.

Paul is telling Timothy to have them stop this. It was poison – getting away from the real purpose of the law. My job as a preacher, like Timothy's job as a preacher, is two-fold: to teach the law and preach the gospel. The Old Testament is the law of Moses – the first five books – and then the rest working it out in practice. The New Testament is the four Gospels of Jesus and then the rest of the New Testament working it out in practice. John Wesley was asked how he was such a successful preacher of the gospel in England and he said: "I ride into a town where I've never been before. I have nothing but a horse between my knees and a Bible in my hands. For the first week I preach nothing but the law. I go through the commands until I notice some people begin to look uncomfortable.... Then I begin to mix just a little gospel with the preaching of the law. Then I mix a little more gospel with the preaching of the law, until finally I am just preaching the gospel. Then they get converted." What a wonderful method!

Preach the law – it awakens conscience; you realise you have broken the law of God, you are wrong with God – then preach the gospel and the love of God that can forgive. The law and the gospel are not against each other, they are partners. As one great preacher in Puritan days use to say, "It is the needle of the law that brings the thread of the gospel into the human heart." Therefore, you must teach the law, but not as an academic thing, a kind of legal exercise.

The Jews used to discuss the law in terms like this: was wearing false teeth on the Sabbath breaking the Sabbath law by carrying a burden? Was wearing a safety pin in your clothes working? If you went for a walk with a stick, that was all right, but if you drag the stick in the dust, wasn't that ploughing and didn't that break the law? You can see how you can have endless fun this way. You can go on discussing details like a lot of lawyers, and you finish up in legalism, which is deadly and has killed fellowships and has killed Christian love.

Now what is the purpose of the law? Why teach it? Paul says that our aim is love. How does preaching the law help love? The answer is: love is the fulfilling of the law. Love says: tell me what God wants me to do and I want to do it. When it hears the Ten Commandments, love will not rebel and react but will say: I want to be like that; that is God's picture for me. Love is the fulfilling of the law because love does not steal and love does not murder. Love gives and love saves; love fulfils the law.

So Paul is teaching that some people were occupying themselves with myths and endless genealogies and promoting speculations rather than the divine training, whereas the aim of our charge is real love. To preach the commandments is to preach love, for love is the fulfilling of the commandments. Now love, if it is going to be real and not sentiment, must have three foundations: a pure heart, a good conscience and a sincere faith. No-one ever really loved until they got those three things. It is the law that will tell you whether you have got a pure heart. It is the teaching of the law that tells you whether you have got a good conscience. It is the teaching of the law that will help you to have a sincere faith, and that is the purpose of the law. It is perverted when it becomes an intellectual exercise. It is doing its job when it leads to a good conscience and a pure heart.

What is a pure heart? In modern language we would say "unmixed motives" – a love that is genuine and that isn't wanting anything out of it. What is a good conscience? I think you know without my having to tell you. What is a sincere faith? Some time ago I came across the origin of the word "sincere". Interestingly, it comes from two Latin words, *sine cera* – in English, "without wax". It comes from the world of secondhand antiques. You may have seen pictures of Roman and Greek statues, and you could buy them. Of course, a statue that was old developed cracks. There were always flaws in marble. You have seen the lines through it – and that may be softer stone, and it may be weathered out, so there is a crack. So a shady dealer would fill up the cracks with white wax. You would not know – you would look at it and think they were the original streaks. Indeed, I recently saw this very thing being done by a builder on some marble. The secondhand dealers used to put up a notice:

"Our Statues are Without Wax" (in Latin, of course). Our statues are *sine cera*, are sincere, are good right through, the genuine article; no patching up, no covering the cracks, really good right through – we haven't been doing this up for the shop window; this is genuine. A sincere faith is not a faith that has waxed up cracks, it is good right through, genuine, the real thing. Now when you have a pure heart that is free from mixed motives, and a good conscience that is free from disobedience, and there is a sincere faith, you are in a position to love and fulfil the law. Why, then, was the law given if love is the fulfilling of the law? If we could get people to love, surely we would not need the law. Yes, that is now what Paul goes on to say. The law is a good thing, it is to reveal and to restrain sin. You don't need laws for good people; you only need them for bad people. God had to give the law to do this.

A Greek philosopher said, "He who does no wrong needs no law." But the tragedy is that we have all done wrong and we need the law to tell us that we have done wrong. We need the law to stop us doing more wrong so that we do not harm other people. Can you imagine what the nation would be like if all the laws were cancelled tomorrow? There would be unrestrained sin, nobody even knowing that they were sinning. So the law is given as one of the two things that God gives to mankind to restrain us in evil and show us when we do wrong. The other thing is conscience. Those are two weapons that God has against evil. One is within and one is outside. Those are the brakes he puts on evil in society. We should thank God for every time conscience has kept us – that little voice inside you that said, "No, this is not the way." Every one of us, I am afraid, would have to say two things: one, that my conscience has sometimes spoken and I have disobeyed it; two, my conscience has sometimes spoken and kept me from doing something that was wrong. Praise God for conscience! A good conscience is a wonderful thing to have. We read later in the chapter of those who shipwrecked their conscience. Religion will always have conscience in it, but conscience by itself is not enough. My conscience is conditioned by my upbringing, by the things I was told were wrong when I was a boy. Therefore my conscience is not altogether a sufficient guide to me. It is amazing how you have conscience about things your parents thought were wrong even if you think they are all right. I will give you an example: I was brought up never to ride a bicycle on Sunday. I do ride one now and I don't feel that it is wrong and I feel that I can justify it in the sight of God. I will tell you when I had to. When I was working on the farm, I was four miles from the nearest church. The only possible way I could get there was on my bicycle. But I remember the first time I rode to church, I felt so guilty. I had never done it before, and I knew I had been told not to. My conscience, in a sense, was conditioned by this, but I got over that. In that sense, I went against my conscience. Why? Because a commandment of God went outside my conscience – overruled it – and the commandment was to worship God.

The conscience needs to be conditioned by the commandments of God. In your early years it is conditioned by the commandments of your earthly father. In your adult years it should be conditioned by your heavenly Father's commandments. A conscience needs re-tuning; it is a good thing but it needs to be brought into line with the commandments of God so that your conscience operates according to that. Just as, for example, the Highway Code was something I had to study when I started driving – that my conscience might come into line with the commands of the Ministry of Transport (at that time). I had to line up my conscience with the commandments of men.

Who are the commandments for? They are for the lawless,

THE PERSONAL LETTERS

the disobedient, the ungodly, sinners, the unholy and the profane. They are not for the religious, not for the godly, not for the holy people—they are for all those other people.

Who else are they for? Paul is running through the Ten Commandments. Murderers of parents – that must be the final act of dishonouring your own father and mother. Some years ago a case was reported of a young man who murdered his own father who had told him he had left his fortune to him in his will. What a horrible act. The law was written for people like that. God had to write laws to restrain murder and manslaughter. Jesus said that you are a murderer if you lose your temper, if you wish anybody dead, if you call them a fool. Then the immoral and the Sodomites are mentioned – "those who are perverted heterosexually or homosexually" is the meaning of the Greek. Also kidnappers, and the worst form of stealing is kidnapping. We hear of those who take hostages. To steal property is bad, but to steal people is a heinous crime and God will call those who do that to answer for it. Where is their conscience? Where is their humanity that they can take people? God had to write laws. He had to make quite clear that these things are wrong and punishable and must be dealt with.

The purpose of the law was to hold the flood of evil back, to show people they are doing wrong, to tell them: this is the fence and if you cross this fence you are trespassing. Without the law you do not even know that you are a sinner.

"Preach sound doctrine." The word "sound" is the same word as in English: hygienic, cleansing, health-giving. So teach hygienic doctrine, clean, healthy doctrine. The law is a sort of medicine, only to be applied where the nature is diseased. Christian teaching is healthy food for healthy people.

Paul has now dealt with the law and said it is good when used against evil but not for intellectual speculation. Now what about the gospel? Paul begins to take off here: "The glorious gospel of the blessed God....." He begins to use adjectives, flowery language, and the thing he can never get over is this: he gave this gospel to me; he entrusted it to my hands. Though I assaulted him, I persecuted him, he gave it to me. Again I think back to a conversation I had with the headmaster of an institution for young offenders. He had real difficulties with one boy, until he said to him, "Will you look after my keys for me?" He handed that unreliable boy the keys of his office cupboards! That dishonest young thief, having been entrusted with those keys, became trustworthy. Paul had insulted and persecuted and was against Christ, sending his followers to prison. Yet Christ had entrusted his gospel to him. The thing that Paul comes to now is the *mercy* that is shown in the gospel. The law can only give you justice, but the gospel gives you mercy – the mercy that lies behind entrusting an enemy with the truth. So he speaks of the mercy shown to him, his gratitude for this mercy, his responsibility to preach, his unworthiness, his ignorance and unbelief before he got the gospel – and his experience with it. The mercy of the Saviour is the thing Paul cannot get over, and now he gives us the summary of Christianity in one sentence: "Christ Jesus came into the world to save sinners."

The religion that we preach is only for sinners. It is not for good people, it is for bad people. The religion that we preach centres in the disease called "sin". Who is the gospel about? It is not about me or you or anyone else, it is about Jesus Christ. Why did he come into the world? He came to save sinners. I know he was a great preacher; I know he was the finest example of human life you will ever find; I know that he healed people, but he didn't come to do any of these things, he came to save sinners. All the other things were by-products of that blessed primary purpose. Our purpose in our churches is to save sinners. If we are not doing that, we are failing in our job. By the grace of Christ we are called to do that. Paul was thinking of this, and that he was the worst sinner in the world – and he was, in the sense that he had been against Christ. Paul affirmed that grace came to him, mercy came to him, and therefore it must mean that God is King. The sovereignty of God, the majesty of the sovereign, is what lay behind the mercy of the Saviour. God's majesty! He decided to take the worst sinner on earth and trust him with the gospel. Only God, the King, could do that.

Why should God choose any of us? Why should he have made me a pastor? I just do not know! It must be the majesty of the sovereign and the mercy of the Saviour together. He must have decided that – as Paul tells his readers of himself: I am an example to others of what God can do with the worst. That is what the gospel is all about. Therefore he finishes this section in v. 17 with a benediction of praise, a doxology. It has been embodied in a wonderful hymn: the King is immortal – always there; invisible – you can't see him but he is really there. The only God – there is no other. To him be honour and glory forever and ever. You only say things like that when you have found the mercy of the Saviour. No one could affirm all that Paul says here unless they had found mercy. It leads to praise.

"Timothy" has a particular meaning: *Timo* means honour, and *theos* means God. Timothy is a name you give to someone who you hope will honour God. Paul is reminding Timothy to give honour to the immortal, invisible, only God. Finally, he says something rather stern, going back to where he started. He says, "Timothy, you must be a good soldier. Wage a good warfare." You notice he doesn't say "Fight a good *battle*", because the Christian life is not a battle; it is a warfare, and warfare is one battle after another. I wish it were true that you could have one big battle and just get over it. I am sure people go to conferences and meetings hoping that they can have one big battle and get it over with and from then on be alright. But saints battle even on their deathbed with evil. It is a warfare which goes on and on. Wage a good warfare, you are a good soldier, hold the faith and have a good conscience. Preach the right thing and practise what you preach. Timothy, be a good soldier but there are two people in your church who are bad sailors – they have shipwrecked their faith. How? By throwing their conscience overboard. By not bringing their conscience into line with the commandments of God.

Let me give the illustration I think Paul had in mind: he is thinking of the conscience as the rudder of the ship. If he were preaching today he could say, "Your conscience is your compass; it must be lined up with the true North which is God's commandments." If you set sail on the Christian life and you throw your compass overboard (or throw your conscience overboard) you have nothing to line up with the commands of God – you will be shipwrecked. The idea that once you become a Christian you finish with conscience is just not true. Christianity must always be a moral thing rather than a mental thing. It is a thing to *do*. Only *think* about it as far as it helps you to *do*. Only talk about the commandments of God insofar as you are prepared to check your compass and see that it is reading true, and then sail following that compass.

"Hymenaeus and Alexander have shipwrecked their faith and I delivered them to Satan that they may learn not to blaspheme." What does Paul mean? To deliver a man to Satan in the New Testament days was to deliver his body to Satan's power that he might become sick, even die, and be stopped from doing what he was doing. It happened to Ananias and Sapphira, It happened to another man whom Paul blinded that he might not be able to go on doing the horrible things he was doing. To deliver a man to Satan is a solemn thing. But Paul was teaching that those two men were teaching others to throw the compass overboard. He had delivered them to Satan, they would fall ill and not be able to mislead people. So serious is wrong teaching that a man is better off ill or dead than poisoning the Christian life of others.

In summary: the commandments of God give you the true North of the Christian's compass, that our consciences might be adjusted and attuned to be reliable guides to us. Then, following a good conscience with a pure heart and a sincere faith, we will love and fulfil the law and it has all been made possible by the mercy of the gospel of our blessed Saviour.

Read 1 Timothy 2

A. DUTY (1–7)
    1. Prayer (1–4)
        a. WHO? Men and their masters
        b. WHY? God and his goodness
    2. Preaching (5–7)
        a. Mediator of the gospel
        b. Messenger to the Gentiles

B. DEMEANOUR (8–15)
    1. Men (8)
        a. Holy hands
        b. Harmonious hearts
    2. Women (9–15)
        a. Seemly adornment
        b. Submissive attitude

There are many things that the Bible doesn't tell you. There are no instructions in it as to how to bake a cake, how to drive a car or build a computer. You have to get all that kind of knowledge from somewhere else. It doesn't even tell you how to get to the moon, but it does tell you how to get to heaven. No scientist on earth has yet discovered any other way, nor will they ever.

There is enough in the Bible to tell us all we need to know about living the Christian life. You don't need any other book than this to learn how to be a Christian and how to continue to walk with Christ. It tells you how to be a Christian in your home, in the intimacies of married life and as parents. It tells you how to be a Christian with that awkward person you work for, with those awkward people you work with or with those awkward people who work for you. Above all, it tells you how to be a Christian in church, which is sometimes the most difficult place to be a Christian, even when you are surrounded by the Lord's people. It is all right provided you don't get too close to each other and just nod and politely say "Good morning" as you come in and go out. But if you really start loving one another and getting close in fellowship, you will discover that all have feet of clay and all of us have awkward corners that need to be knocked off. Living together in fellowship is what Christ has called us to.

The pastoral letters are concerned with living together in church as Christians so that people can say, "See how these Christians love each other." First of all, Paul deals with our worship, the services we hold. He deals with two things: first our *duty* – what we ought to do by way of prayer and preaching; then, secondly, our *demeanour*, which is as important as our duty. We have a duty to pray, we have a duty to preach but there is also demeanour, which concerns such things as men's hands and women's dress. The Bible has quite a lot to say about this. Indeed, it is quite a study to look at what the Bible says about fashion. But we are going to look at the men and the women and their demeanour in worship.

The two key words in the first part of this chapter are "all" and "one". We are going to look at the inclusive nature of Christianity and the exclusive nature. Our prayer must be inclusive of all people but exclusive and about one man: the man Christ Jesus – about the one God and the one mediator. This is the contrast: we are exhorted to live on a big map, not to forget a single member of the human race, billions though there are, and to pray for them. We cannot pray for them by name, but we can at least pray for all people and include the world in its desperate need in our prayers and not just pray for "me, my aunt, and my children."

Paul uses some interesting words for prayer in 2:1 – *supplication*, *prayer* and *intercession*. He is not just piling up the words, every one is significant. Only beggars say, "I've got nothing to eat – will you give me something? I've got nothing to wear – can you spare an old coat?" Only beggars *supplicate*, and the kind of prayer that God loves to hear is the prayer of a beggar. George Bernard Shaw said that forgiveness is a beggar's refuge. I don't care! I am a beggar and you are a beggar because forgiveness is the one thing we cannot find for ourselves. You don't come to church to patronise the church or God – you come as a beggar. We may have nice clothes, we may have had a good breakfast, but for spiritual food we are beggars. Unless God gives us something to eat, we go away hungry. As far as our spiritual clothes go, we are in rags, naked, so the first note in prayer ought to be a note of *supplication*. We are begging God for something because we will find it nowhere else. Make your supplications – there is a sense of need here.

The second word, *prayer*, is something that is never offered to people. You ask people for things, but to ask God for something is different. When you say, "God, could I please have this," you are praying. You are coming to him. The third word used here, *intercessions*, is used exclusively of a petition presented to a king. To intercede was a word kept in the ancient world for going to a throne. So, when you come to pray, remember that you are a beggar coming to a throne. That is a concept of prayer that will get us in the right mood and teach us the right words, giving us the right attitude and spirit. I am a beggar standing before the King, yet he says, "What do you want? What can I give you? What can I do for you?"

Then notice another word Paul uses for prayers: *thanksgivings*. Let the cycle of prayer go the whole circle. You have supplicated, you have begged, and God will give. Return to God in thanksgiving. The only thing that you and I can ever give to him is thanks. We have nothing else to give. Everything that I have he gave to me first. But my thanks to him is something that he didn't give me first – I can give that to him from me alone.

Like every minister, I would get beggars coming to the door. You probably get them too – people coming up to you in the street and begging. I can only recall one, I think, who ever came back and said thank you. Jesus healed ten lepers and one of them said "thank you". This is the cycle of prayer: *please*; *thank you* – "please", that things may flow down from the throne to the beggar; "thank you" – flowing up from the beggar to the throne. That is how we pray, not just for ourselves but for everybody in the world.

We are to pray for all people and their masters. We are to pray for kings and leaders – whether they be Christian or not. By the time Paul wrote this it is likely that the emperor was Nero, under whom, probably, Paul was to have his head chopped off, but Paul calls for prayer for that man. When the early Christians were told to bow down and worship the emperor they would say: I will not worship the Emperor, but I promise to pray for him.

Those set in authority today are not the kings and queens. There are very few of them left anyway, and those that are have little power. Nowadays Presidents, Prime Ministers and others are leading figures. But we do not worship them or international organisations. Athough we know that until the Prince of peace comes the world cannot have peace, we pray for those set in authority. Why? Because the gospel can be furthered in peace and people can live godly and quiet lives in peace. War shatters and disturbs. It cuts countries off from the gospel. In many church buildings there is a tablet with the names on it of casualties, those who went away to wars and did not come back. I wanted to have another memorial tablet for those who went to war and came back spiritually dead. Thousands of men in Britain went to church until they went to war, and came back having seen such godless and terrible things they did not return to church. One man told me, honestly, "I don't feel I can face God after what I had to do in the war." We are told to pray for those who can bring a measure of peace – so that frontiers may be open, and hot and cold wars may be neutralised so that the gospel may spread and all people may come to the truth. You certainly cannot send missionaries through a war. It disrupts the spread of the gospel; it sets up barbed wire barriers between people. So we are to pray for peace that we may live godly and quiet lives. You could say to me, "Well, peace doesn't bring that." I know it doesn't – in peace you have the leisure and the luxury to live low standards of morality. Therefore, it is not enough just to pray for the peace of the world. It is important to go on and to preach the truth in that peace. The reason why we should pray for all people is that God in his goodness desires all to be saved. Let it never be said in the name of Christ that God only wants a few to be saved. The Bible does not say that. My Bible tells me that, "It is not the pleasure of the Lord that the wicked should die. God wants all men to be saved." That translation is a good deal more accurate than the Authorised Version, which has, "who *wills* all men to be saved." When people have read that, they have sometimes said, "If God wills it, it must happen, and therefore everybody is going to be saved anyway and we don't need to be worried about those who are going to be lost." That is a travesty of scripture. The word here is not the strong word "wills" in the sense of "decrees", but "desires; wants". Let us tell everybody: "God wants you to be saved." Let's tell anybody who will listen: "God wants you in heaven." It is our solemn duty to do so. I know that it is a lovely truth taught in scripture, and I believe it, that God chose us in Christ from before the foundation of the world, but he never intended that truth to prevent us from saying that he desires all people to come to the knowledge of him.

That takes me from prayer to preaching. If our prayer is to be as wide as that, and inclusive of the whole human race, our preaching must be as narrow as this: *There is one God and there is one mediator between man and God, the man Christ Jesus, who gave himself a ransom for all*. That is a summary of what I believe and preach. First of all, there is one God. Someone who says there is no God is lying. Someone who says (as many people believe) that there are two gods, one good and one bad, is lying. Anyone who says there are many gods that you have got to keep happy is not telling the truth. People who are kept in the darkness of believing that there is no God or many gods need to come to a knowledge of the truth. There is one and only one God. Let us realise again that this puts the lid on any idea that all religions are much the same and that it does not matter which one you adopt. There is only one God and he is Yahweh.

A girl talking to me about church unity said, "There's no real difference between us, we pray to the same God – you pray through Jesus, I pray through Mary." To her there is one God and one mediator: Mary.

"But Mary can't be a mediator for me," I replied. "Why do you pray to Mary?"

"Well, if I want anything out of my dad I always get my mum to get round him." It sounded quite logical to her! So I had to say that our heavenly Father is not like her earthly father. There is only one mediator, one person who can get you through to the only God who exists, and his name is Jesus.

Here are two reasons why he can get you through, why he is the only mediator, and why Christianity is therefore exclusive and you will only get to God through Jesus who declared, "No-one comes to the Father but by me." First, Jesus is the only person who is both God and man. It is so obvious. I need a mediator who is God, and can talk to God, and who is man and who understands me. I need a mediator who is not someone vaguely in between, but someone who is both – who knows what it is to be divine, and is divine, and who knows what it is to be human, and who understands. If Mary understands me because she is human, she is not divine, not God. It is because Jesus is uniquely God and man that he can bring his hands together with me in them, and there I am with God. Indeed, to talk to Jesus is to get through to the Father. Secondly, I need someone who will mediate for me with God, someone who will be the go-between, who will speak to God on behalf of poor old JDP. How can I get that? Jesus knows me, and here is the other reason: *he gave his life a ransom for all*. No other person did that for me. When he goes to the Father he pleads not me but himself. The hands he lifts up to God the Father are pierced hands *for me*.

What does this word "ransom" mean? Literally, it is an exchange person, an exchange price. What Jesus did for me makes him unique as a mediator. He can say to the Father: accept me as a hostage instead of this man. Nobody else can mediate like that. I have a mediator right there where he is needed, taking my place, speaking for me, and setting me free.

That is my preaching. We have a duty to pray for all people, of all colours and all races, and our prayer must be as wide as that. But in our preaching I say there is only one man can help you, the man Christ Jesus. Don't forget that he is still a man. I have a job persuading unbelievers that he is God, but I have a job persuading believers that he is man still. Jesus has a human body still. He is still a human being. We don't have a high priest untouched with our infirmities, but he understands. To have a human being in heaven who is divine and a Saviour is all you need. My heart bleeds when I talk to people who are trusting another human being to get them through to God – whether a live human being or a dead one – trying to get through to God through someone else. There is only one God and there is only one way to that one God – Jesus.

Paul had been appointed a preacher to the Gentiles – to anybody, the outcasts, the untouchable, the people beyond the pale, those of whom it was thought they would never belong to God. He uses three words about himself — preacher, apostle, teacher. A preacher is someone with an announcement to make; an apostle was someone who had been sent by a king to give an announcement; a teacher is someone who instructs in the truth.

So much for our duty. Our demeanour is also important. It

matters how you dress when you go to church, though not in the way that society often thinks. It matters how you behave in church, though I am glad we have moved away from some of the rather rigid formality. The order that we have must be the order of life, not the order of death. But nevertheless there is guidance in scripture as to how to behave in church, first of all for the men. Funnily enough, we are told here of a posture for prayer. It is not to kneel, not to stand, but to do something with your hands. In the Bible they prayed holding out their hands – how expressive, and it is the natural gesture when you are asking for something, like that of a child who says, "Please can I have this." Lifting up hands is the most natural gesture in the world. May I suggest that you might like to try it? It will help you to realise you are asking for something from a King and you are praying.

We are to pray with *holy* hands. A minister of a church who had been a heavy smoker came to me once and said, "David, I've given up smoking."

I asked him, "Well, what made you do that?"

He replied, "It was last Sunday morning. The people came to the communion rail, they knelt down and I took white bread and gave them each a piece. I suddenly noticed how brown my fingers were and I felt I just couldn't use hands like that to give the Body of Christ to people, so I've stopped smoking." That was very practical. If you are going to lift your hands up to God they have to be clean. Now what does Paul mean? I remember vividly as a boy, my mother saying, "Have you washed your hands?" If you are coming to ask for food from God, it is not so important that they should be washed with water and soap. Jesus didn't really set great store by that. He was criticised for eating meals without washing his hands first. But we are told of "holy hands", meaning hands that are wholly dedicated to him, hands that are going to do things for him during the week. They may be hardened hands, but then Jesus' hands were – he had made chairs and tables for a long time. But they were holy hands, that wouldn't bodge a job. They were hands that offered their work to God. They were hands that were going to handle things that would help, and his hands were hands that would heal and touch. Have you ever studied the verses in scripture referring to the hands of Christ? It is a wonderful thing – he laid his hands on people; he touched them.

Men lift up hands, but they must be hands that are going to do the right thing during the week. With your hands you can do wrong things. Lift up holy hands and have hearts of harmony. One translation renders the next phrase "without anger or argument".

When we pray, we are to avoid preaching in prayer. It is terribly easy to have anger or argument in your heart when you pray. I remember hearing of one prayer when a man said, "Lord, heap coals of fire on my enemy's head, I'd love to see him burn" – which was a very frank and honest prayer, but I think a misinterpretation of scripture. When we pray, we are to lift up hands without argument, disputation. Prayer is not the place to disagree. We are not praying to people or praying against them, we are praying to God. Holy hands and hearts of harmony – that is enough for the men.

There is only one verse for the men and about five for the women, so I am following Paul. What about the women? It seems to me that in the New Testament the women took part in public worship, but there were limits to the part they took. It seems to be quite clear that they prayed and they prophesied. 1 Corinthians 11 tells us that, but we see they were not allowed to teach (which is what we call preaching today, but is in fact teaching). Now this was the line drawn. Therefore, when Paul says, "The women also" or "likewise", it seems to me that he is thinking of them praying too. That is what the word "also" means. The men should pray like this and the women *also*. But he does not tell them about their hands or their hearts, he tells them about certain other things.

Before we plunge into these dangerous and difficult waters, let me make some general points. I know that many women don't like Paul. I know that because whenever I preach what he says they don't like me either! Paul's views on women in the church have been criticised and dismissed on three grounds. First of all, there are some who say his attitude was purely psychological – that he was a bachelor, and a women-hating bachelor, and that you can see his psychology coming out. I think that is a libel, for there is not a shred of evidence in the New Testament about this. He had some wonderful women colleagues: Euodia, Syntyche, Lois, Eunice, Priscilla. It is very interesting to notice that Peter, who was married, wrote exactly the same things as Paul says here. So you are not going to get away with suggesting that Paul was psychologically unbalanced.

Secondly, there are those who say: "Paul was simply a child of his day. They kept women down in those days and he was just reflecting the views of the people around him, and we have grown out of this. At the very highest, he was still terribly Jewish in outlook." I don't believe that either. If that were true then we can throw out most of what Paul said as simply being from a child of his day.

Thirdly, there are those who say: "He said what he did about women because of the social conditions then," that he was simply saying something that applied then in the conditions of society at that time, but does not apply today. I do not see all that much difference between society today and society then, if you read Romans 1.

It is really a test, to me, of your belief in the inspiration of scripture. Is this the word of the Lord or is it not? Is Paul giving his own ideas or is the Lord speaking through him? Firstly, in Christ, Paul taught that there is no difference of *status*. Neither Jew nor Greek, male nor female, bond nor free – no difference in status. Secondly, he employed women in gospel service. Thirdly, he commends many women for their qualities. Fourth, he recommends marriage and he praises wives and mothers. Fifthly, he has the highest view of women. I could give you many quotes: 1 Corinthians 7, 1 Corinthians 11, Ephesians 5 – we see a very high view of women. Do you tell me that a man is a woman-hater who says there is no difference in status, who employs women in gospel service, who commends them, who recommends marriage and who upholds womanhood in every possible way? No, but in the modern world the roles have been reversed. If we are not careful, what we are doing is reflecting our society instead of reflecting God's word. It is a question of which is going to govern us. Is it the world in which we live or the word which we read?

Paul mentioned two things about women in church. First of all: seemly adornment. A man bolder than I said, "A woman's dress is a mirror of her mind." He singles out hairstyle, jewellery, and clothes. Two things he condemns in connection with these three. One: expense, two: exhibitionism—that's all. Exhibitionism is the brazen flaunting of self and expense: the spending of far too much money in these three realms. Pliny, a Roman official, tells of a wedding he attended where the dress cost what in our money would be more than half a million pounds! But I don't think there were many women as wealthy as that in the early church. There are two extremes to avoid: ostentatious extravagance and careless dowdiness. Paul teaches that real beauty is not what you put on but what you give out. It is not what you do to yourself, it is what you do to others. Let your beauty be that of good works, as befits those who profess godliness. I know that is the secret of real beauty. The Methodist Dr Sangster held a beauty queen competition in his church, which may shock you. But there was one qualification: every entrant had to be over sixty years of age, and he did it to prove that real beauty is not skin deep but something much deeper – it comes out.

Now the other thing, which is even more unpopular, is a submissive attitude. Their part in public assembly is to learn rather than to teach, to be humble and deferent. Now this sounds pretty rough to some. In fact, brides today often refuse to say the word "obey" when they get married. Paul gives two reasons and I simply pass them on to you because he finds them not in society but in the very word of God in the beginning. Here are the two reasons: woman was created second and sinned first. For those reasons it becomes her nature to let the men have the authority in the assembly. Why should this be? Take the first: created second. God did not create woman to be man's competitor, but man's companion. What lovely companions they make, but what poor competitors. I mean by this that God, when he created us male and female, had a reason for doing so. It was not to create two kinds of team, to see which team could get on top. It was to create partners. There are things that my wife can do that I cannot do, and things that I can do that she can't. God made us to be partners.

I am reminded of the famous punster who was approached by a woman who thought herself in every way able to cope with what a man does. She said to him, "Can you think of any essential difference between you and me?" He said, "Madame, I cannot conceive" – which was a clever answer. Woman was made to bring up children, to create a home and family, and to glorify God – but not exclusively – there are other ministries of women who don't get married that are lovely ministries to people; there is intuition, sensing a need where a man like me just couldn't. I remember years ago visiting a dear old soul and I was talking to her, as ministers do. One of the church members came into the sickroom, a lady who was also visiting. She went straight to the bed, lifted up the patient, puffed the pillow up and just put it down a few inches. I would never have done that – I would not have noticed it. A man would just have sat and talked. But a woman came in, saw a ministry and did what was needed. Let us recognise the function: equal status but different functions. We are partners, and this is our calling.

Not that women haven't a ministry of speaking to people about the Lord, of praying, and of so much else as well, but let us remember that God created us for particular functions. Woman was created second but she did sin first; she was deceived. It is devilish to deceive a woman and it is easier to do so than to deceive a man. It is wise in the assembly for men to teach and have the authority.

"Yet woman will be saved through bearing children if she continues in faith and love and holiness, with modesty." I have come across many different interpretations of this verse. One suggests that childbirth atones for her sins – but that would be a contradiction of the gospel. Another is that she will be kept safe through childbearing – yet that does not always happen. Or that she will be saved even though she must bear children—but I think that does not really fit into scripture either. Some even say that this means she will be saved through the birth of the child Christ Jesus. But it took a midwife to tell me what this verse really means. She said, "You know, I understand that verse." Having read all the books of scholars who disagreed about it, I thought: now I am on to it. I asked, "What do you mean?"

She answered me, "You know when a woman is bearing a child and I'm by the bed, she's going through the pain – and yet the hope and expectancy! All the fears of things going wrong and yet all the hopes of things going right. When she is going through that and is creating life, she gets very near to God. Very often, women whom I have visited who have never mentioned religion, call on God sincerely at that time. They are near to reality, near to life, near to death, and they are so near that they call on God."

She continued, "I have known women who because of that experience sought God later and went on to know the Lord. But, I've also known a lot who didn't continue. When the crisis was over, they got so wrapped up in their family again that they didn't go on."

Does that not fit? Women will be saved through childbearing if they continue in faith and love and holiness, with modesty. In other words, there is an experience which is a unique reminder of reality, of life, of creation, of God and of death – an experience which could bring a woman to put her trust in God, and go on and continue in that.

Read 1 Timothy 3

A. SUPERVISORS (1–7) – "elders"
  1. Incentive (1)
  2. Instructions (2–7)
    a. Personal (2–3)
      i. Positive – integrity innocence insight invitation instruction
      ii. Negative – alcoholic aggressive argumentative acquisitive
    b. Domestic (4–5)
    c. Mature (6)
    d. Social (7)

B. SERVANTS (8–13) – deacons/deaconesses
  1. Instructions (8–11)
    a. Men (8–10)
      i. Serious ii. Straight iii. Sober
      iv. Satisfied v. Sound vi. Stable
    b. Women (11)
      i. Serious ii. Silent iii. Sober iv. Stable
  2. Incentive (12-13)
    a. Among men – standing in the church
    b. Towards God – confident in the faith

Postscript (14–16)
    a. Household of God
      i. Church of the living God
      ii. Pillar and bulwark of the truth
    b. Head in glory
      i. Begins with birth, finishes with ascension
      ii. Manifested in flesh, vindicated by Spirit
      iii. Seen by angels, believed by men

I came across these words: The church is a gritty and granular collection of pious particles." Another commentator said: "The Church is the disease of Christianity." I meet many people today who feel that Christianity would be better without the church – that if we all just followed Christ and got rid of the church we would get on very well. I have some sympathy with that outlook, especially if anyone has had unfortunate experience in a church. But then I ask, "Well, who thought of having a church anyway? Whose idea was it? Was it just a group of clergymen with a vested interest in their own careers? The answer is: God thought of it, and the Lord Jesus did. The church was his idea. The notion that you can be a Christian without being part of a church is nonsense for the simple reason that to say you are a Christian means that you believe in Christ, that you follow him, and that at the very least you want to do what he said. It was he who said "I will build my church", so you cannot claim to follow him unless you are interested in the church.

That leads me to another point. If it was God's idea to have a church, do you think that he would have left us to decide what kind of a church we ought to have? Do you think he would have left the organisation, the pattern of his church, to us? If he said, "I will build my church," do you think he would have said, "Well, you can plan it. You can have it how you will. You can arrange it how you want"? Never. That is why in the Bible we are not only told to be in the church, we are told what sort of a church to be in. We are not only told to be part of the fellowship, we are told how to behave in the household of God, what ministry we ought to have, what officers we ought to have. That is why 1 Timothy is in the New Testament. Should we have bishops? Should we have archbishops? Should we have popes? Should

THE PERSONAL LETTERS

we have cardinals? Should we have area superintendents? Should we have ministers? Should we have "Reverends", "Right Reverends" and "Most Reverends"? What should we have? If Jesus has a church, what kind of a ministry does he want that church to have? What kind of leaders, what kind of officers? Does he, for example, want the kind of church where only one man is ministering? So that people use that horrid phrase, "Mr So-and-So's church"? What is his will and pattern? We learn about this in 1 Timothy chapter 3.

But first look at one verse in Philippians, 1:1. "Paul and Timothy,"—they were together there, "servants of Christ Jesus to all the saints in Christ Jesus who are at Philippi with the bishops and deacons." In other words, a pattern emerges from the New Testament in which there are two kinds of officer or leader in the church: bishops and deacons. Now whether it is safe to use the word "bishops" today in this context will remain to be seen. It could be very misleading today, because it could mean that we might think that a group of men in each church ought to dress up in robes and wear rings, which of course the New Testament says nothing whatever about. But one thing is patently obvious. First of all, a church needs two sorts of official, two sorts of officer: bishops (whatever that means) and deacons (whatever that means). Furthermore, it is quite obvious that every church needs more than one of both of these kinds of people. Every church in every place needs bishops (plural) and deacons (also plural). Indeed, this is the pattern of ministry right through the New Testament. There are no such things as one-man ministries, even in missionary work. Jesus sent them out in twos. When Paul went on a missionary journey, he went with Barnabas or Timothy or Mark. It was always a shared team. If we go away from that pattern into individualist activity, we can expect problems.

Let us look at the actual titles, then the functions, then the authority, and finally the qualifications given to these two groups of people needed by every church.

There are two words in the Greek language of the New Testament translated by the word "bishop" in English. One is the word *episcopos*, from which we get our word "episcopal". The other is the word *presbuteros*, which gives us our word "Presbyterian". The Greek word deacon is *diakonos*, which is much the same as the English word. The word *presbuteros* means elder and another word used of deacon, *neotoras*, means younger, so that you could call these two groups of people the elders and the youngers. Or you could give them another name. You could give them the word "overseer", because the word *episcopos* meant in the ancient world "foreman" – a man who has more experience than the others, therefore, he is elder than the others in the sense of his trade. The word does not mean old, it means elder. This does not mean that God wants the church run by old men. But it does mean that he wants the church to be in the hands of foremen who are more experienced than the others in the things of God – elders. He also wants deacons who are there to serve.

Where did this pattern come from? Did God think it up? Funnily enough, no – he was adopting a pattern that was there in society already. If we use the word "elder", here are some interesting facts. The Spartans were governed by a group of people called the *gerusia*, from which we get the word "geriatric". That is the simple meaning of the word "elder". The Romans were governed by a senate, and the word "senate" is the same root word as our word "*senile*" – it meant "older people". In England we have had "aldermen" in some local councils, meaning older, more experienced men, senior men, those who can advise and help. So Roman society and Greek society had elders—mature people who were foremen in society.

THE PERSONAL LETTERS

Furthermore, the Jewish synagogues had elders. Of course, elders started way back in the days of Moses. When the people of Israel came out of Egypt they were a one-man ministry. They had one minister, Moses. It was Jethro, Moses' father-in-law who suggested he needed somebody else to help him manage. Since his church numbered two and a half million, I think this was fairly good advice from Moses' father-in-law! So Moses appointed elders, senior men, foremen of the people of God to help with the task of leading them through their pilgrimage.

In the synagogues there were always a group of elders. Do you know that in Jewish synagogues, you couldn't start one (and you still can't) until you have got at least twelve men meeting together for worship. You certainly couldn't start a synagogue with twelve ladies. There must be twelve men so that you have at least some elders out of those men to be foremen of the synagogue. From those elders, one would be called the teaching elder or, in Hebrew, "rabbi". So the pattern of the synagogue was rabbi plus elders, men who led the synagogue of God.

Then, even before the New Testament, the synagogues had deacons. The deacons were in charge of the "box". They went round with it and collected money which they took to the needy and distributed (hence, our "Boxing Day").

In the New Testament, God is revealing that he wants the church run on the same pattern, so that everything is done decently and in order, with a group of men who are foremen, elders, overseers – who are *episcopoi*, *presbuteroi*, bishops—call them what you will, but a group of men in each fellowship who are elders to look after the youngers; and a group of deacons – the word meaning to serve, to look after the practical side.

The first English Baptist church started in Amsterdam in the year 1612, among a number of English refugees

1 TIMOTHY 3

who had fled from the totalitarian religion of England, and ultimately fled from Holland to America with the Pilgrim Fathers. I have a copy of the book containing the statement that they made about what they believed as a church. Here is one sentence from it: "We believe that the officers of every church or congregation are either elders, who by their office do especially feed the flock concerning their souls, or deacons – men and women who by their office relieve the necessities of the poor and impotent brethren, concerning their bodies." That is a lovely, clear statement, which is right in line with the New Testament. God wants a church to have elders and deacons because people have souls and bodies—the elders will look after people's souls, the deacons their bodies.

These are such distinct and different callings that in Acts chapter 6 a very clear principle is laid down in an event in the early church dividing these two ministries among two different sorts of Christian. It arose because somebody was grumbling about the church catering. They provided food for widows who had nowhere to go for a meal. Some widows were grumbling that others were getting better helpings and getting there first, and so on. They came to the apostles, who were the elders of the early church. Seeing that something was not right, the apostles said, "It is not right for us to leave our spiritual ministry, prayer, ministering the word and preaching, to come and be busy serving tables. Look out from among you seven men full of the Holy Spirit who can be set apart for this practical work." They did, and they chose Stephen, Philip, and a number of others and made them deacons. From then on, serving tables became the business of those deacons. Incidentally, it is very interesting that they chose men – serving tables was in the hands of men in those days.

Here was the clear distinction between the spiritual and

THE PERSONAL LETTERS

the physical needs of the church of Christ. It will always have both because people are bodies as well as souls and a church is interested in the whole person. A church cannot just say it is only interested in saving souls. We should be interested in the welfare of bodies too.

What is the authority of these two groups of people? This is the most ticklish question of all. The word *episcopos* or elder or bishop, or whatever you call these people, implies that they superintend others. A foreman superintends those who are doing a job. He doesn't call them all together and say, "Now what should we be doing?" He doesn't ask them to take a vote on what he should be doing as foreman. He is a foreman, an elder. He is in that position to lead others and tell them what needs to be done. So first it is quite impossible to have elders in a church where the members say, "We decide everything" because an elder could not be an elder under those circumstances if every decision he made was subject to the vote of the workmen. Of course elders are not dictators. A foreman has a double responsibility. He has a responsibility to the employer or anybody above him to do the job. An elder is responsible to the Lord for the way he does his job. Secondly, a foreman does have a responsibility to those beneath him. The responsibility is to give them proper leadership, to give them the right answer when they bring a problem, to be there and ready. He is not to do what those under him tell him, but to do what those above him tell him. Therefore, in the New Testament there are frequent exhortations to accept the rule of the elders, to believe that God has given them to be foremen, that the church might be well-run. The church does not run well when it is run either as a democracy or a dictatorship. If it is a dictatorship, or the minister, or one man, or one family is telling everybody else what to do, it does not run at all well. Nor does it run well when the members tell the leaders what

1 TIMOTHY 3

to do. God meant the church to be run in a businesslike way, with foremen responsible to him leading the fellowship in what needs to be done, but doing it responsibly. For just as a foreman can be sacked, so God can remove an elder from his position if he is not doing well.

What about the deacons? What is their position in relationship to the church? If elders are set over the church by God, deacons are set under the church by God, so it is not a kind of hierarchy—bishops, deacons, members. It is in fact bishops or elders, members, deacons. A deacon is someone who serves. He is called to be a servant, to do what is needed by the members. So if the members desire or decide that it is right to do something with money, then the deacons are told, "Here is something that needs to be done. Will you do it?"

In other words, elders are over the church of God, deacons are under it – and that is the divine pattern. Not that deacons should be servile or subservient, because service is a great privilege. When Jesus took a towel and washed feet he did not say, "I don't like being under you." He was still their Lord and Master, but he served – he got down and did something that somebody below them should have done. Here, then, is the pattern.

Do you realise that in every normal family this is the pattern? Not that anybody considers themselves superior to anybody else, but in a normal family, under God, the father is the bishop, the elder, the leader, and the mother is the deacon, and the children are the members. In the right family in the right setting, this is the pattern of God. The same pattern you see in a family, in a synagogue, in a Roman senate or in a Greek city is the pattern that God wants in the church – deacons and elders.

The first seven verses are all about elders, and I am going to use the word "elder" or "superintendent" from now on because I do think the word "bishop" has a different connotation. "Bishop" now means one man over many churches, and that is not what we are thinking of here. This concerns many bishops over one church. The first thing we are told here is that it is a good thing to have an ambition to be an elder. There is a kind of false modesty that would say, "Oh, you must never think of being a leader. You ought to scramble for the back seat – that is true humility." But here is the Word of God saying that if you would like to be an elder, that's a noble task. It is a good ambition. Here is one of the incentives to be an elder. As Moffat translates this: it is an excellent occupation. Indeed, every man in the church ought to have an ambition, I think, to be an elder, a desire to be chosen by God to be a foreman – to be a man who could help others to do the job. But, lest you rush into it, here are the qualifications. I tremble when I read this. They really are very strong qualifications. If you are going to have a foreman over the church, he must be qualified in many ways – positive and negative. Let us take the personal qualifications first: a man of integrity, irreproachable; a man who, one version says, "married only once". There is a debate about the meaning of this phrase. It either means married once or married to one wife. I think on the whole my understanding would tend to the second. What is quite clear is that his marriage must be according to God's pattern. This particularly applies of course in other parts of the world, but it also applies to a degree here. He must be temperate in his habits – sober, sensible, and dignified. That is a very nice little trio. He must be a man of insight, with a safe and sound mind, a man whose home is open to people who come with needs because so much of his work will be done at the fireside rather than in the pulpit; a man who is able to instruct others in the faith and apt to teach.

On the negative side, he must not be alcoholic, aggressive, argumentative or acquisitive. He must not be an alcoholic, though it does not say he mustn't drink. Wine was the normal drink, and in this very letter Paul tells Timothy to take a little wine for his stomach's sake – but he must not be an alcoholic, a drunkard. Why? Because he must be a man of self-control. He must not be aggressive, literally "a fist user". You may think that could not happen but it has happened. A man must not be a fist fighter. You don't settle arguments in the church that way! He must not be argumentative; he must not be acquisitive, he certainly must not be a man who is out for all he can get and loves money.

Those are the personal qualifications. What about the domestic ones? If he can't manage his own family he certainly can't be an elder. That's frightening, particularly when children reach the teens. What it tells us is this: I have sat in a law court and heard a mother say of a nine year old child, "I just can't do anything with him." Well, if you can't manage your own children whom God has put under your care all the time, how can you possibly be an elder over the children of God's family? This is one of the keys to whether a man can be a foreman – whether he can manage, whether he can rule and govern within the more limited sphere of his own family circle, and have the respect of his children too.

His spiritual qualifications are that he must not be a new Christian, a recent convert. Or else it might go to his head that he, in his Christian youth as it were, is leading others. Therefore we are to wait until a man has gone on with the Lord lest he fall into the snare of the devil. What was the snare of the devil? He got a bit proud and a bit big and he stepped out of his place in glory. A man can go the way of the devil if things go to his head if he is appointed too soon. Socially, he must be not popular in the world outside but *respected*. Unbelievers must be able to say, "Well, I don't like him but I respect him," or even, "I do like him." But we are not told that we ought to be universally popular. "Woe unto you if all men speak well of you." But we are told that people outside the church should say, "He is a Christian, I can see that." Again, the danger is that the devil can get hold of you if people outside don't see that.

Now let us turn to the deacons (verses 8–13) and here we notice straightaway that deacons can be men or women. Elders are always men. Fathers are always men in a family and foremen in the church are men, but deacons are men and women. The men are dealt with in verses 8–10 and from v. 11 onwards the women likewise. Now the Authorised Version has "wives" but it seems very clear that it is the women because the Bible speaks about deaconesses. There is one mentioned in Romans 16:1 – I commend to you our sister Phoebe, a deaconess....

What are deacons to be? First of all they are to be serious. A deacon who is always cracking jokes and being silly is a bit of an anomaly. You need a sense of humour to be a deacon, but nevertheless a deacon must be straight in what he says, so that when he says yes he means yes, and when no he means no, a man who is sober in his habit and content with his money. This is important. You realise that Judas was a deacon. Judas was a treasurer, and the treasurer of the apostles was too fond of money and you know where that ended, in suicide. It is a warning to us all that when we handle the money of God we need men who are content with their possessions, and that is very important.

Sound in doctrine – it is interesting that if you are going to serve tables and handle money you must be sound in doctrine and hold the faith. Sometimes people might think that you can have someone doing these practical jobs who is not even yet a Christian. Sometimes people say, "Well, give him this job, it will bring him into things." But until a person is a Christian and believes the faith he should not be handling even God's money, or tables, or anything practical.

He should be stable in his service so it is wise to put him on probation as a deacon for a time and at the end of that to say, "Yes, you make a good deacon" – but having tested him first. Only four things are said about the deaconesses. They are to be serious, which does not mean always grave. They are to be silent when they need to be. That is mentioned quite deliberately here: not gossips, not slanderers. They are to be sober and stable, absolutely trustworthy.

Paul adds, in verses 12–13, an incentive to be a deacon. You should *want* to be a deacon or a deaconess – it should be an ambition. Why? For two reasons: first of all, you will gain standing in the church, and second, you will gain confidence in the faith. Once again people might say, "Paul, you're not being very Christian." Telling church members that they will gain a good standing in the church is a right and proper thing. Wouldn't you like to have a good standing in the church? What is a good standing? It is to be a pillar, and that is to hold people up. I suppose in any church, if you took the membership roll and went through it, you could take certain people and say, "They are pillars. They are holding the thing up." If you took those people out, the thing would go. Thank God for those who have got this good standing because people look to them, they support others, and it is a fine thing to have a good standing in a church. The other incentive is that you will have much more confidence in the faith. One translation says that you will have the right to speak openly on matters of the Christian faith. Why? Because you are a pillar of the church, you can speak with some authority now. You are in good standing and you will have confidence to speak boldly of the faith of Jesus Christ.

We can sum up this section by pointing out three things. Firstly, in all these qualifications there is not one mention of any natural talents. Isn't that wonderful? You don't need natural talents to be an elder or a deacon. All you need are spiritual talents, which God can give to anyone. Therefore I do not care what your education has been, what your bank balance is or whether you are cultured or not. God can choose anyone to be an elder or a deacon. Isn't that lovely? A church should demonstrate this. A church should be able to show that any man can be called of God to be an elder. Any man or woman can be made a deacon or a deaconess. They do not have to be rich or educated; they do need to be all that God wants them to be.

Secondly, the same spiritual qualifications come for both elders and deacons. The qualifications for deacons who are going to do practical work is that they should be spiritual. Woe betide a church where the elders are all the spiritual men and the deacons are the unspiritual men. Sooner or later there is going to be a tug of war between elders and deacons. But when they are all spiritual, the machine works. Thirdly, there is not an impossible standard in either of these two offices. Everything mentioned is within reach of a believer who will allow the Holy Spirit to work with them. Not that everybody will be an office-holder – God will give gifts and call some. But he can give these things to anyone.

Thirdly, there is a little postscript (v. 15). Paul says, "I am writing this down so that you may know how one ought to behave in the household of God." A church that says "We believe the Bible to be God's Word" is a church that must behave according to it. It is not really an optional extra, whether you have these kinds of ministry. If you claim to be in the household of God, this is how you behave.

Most early Baptist churches had elders and deacons but towards the end of the nineteenth century the elders began to shrink from many to few, and to one. About the turn of the century, the elder began to be called "Reverend" and turn his collar back to front. The pattern was one elder and many deacons. It soon became patently obvious that one man cannot carry the responsibility for matters of membership and spiritual concern. So the development that then took place is that the deacons then began to share again with the minister in the spiritual ministry of the church. But then that produced the anomalous situation that now you elect the same people to do both jobs, and their meetings must cover both, and they haven't the time nor have all the gifts to do so. There are many Baptist churches today which are going back and saying, "You know, God was right after all." This is surely the pattern: a bunch of elders with a teaching elder, rabbi, reverend, whatever you'd like to call him – but a teaching elder among elders looking after the flock spiritually as foremen, leaders. A group of deacons should be dedicated to looking after the needs of the poor and powerless and all the material needs of buildings, finance, welfare and the rest of it.

Finally, in the postscript Paul is teaching that the setting for all this is that the church is the household of God and must be well-run for this reason: that it is the pillar and bulwark of the truth. We are in the business of conveying the truth to people. Therefore, we must be a well-run organisation. This is God's pattern for a church that is well-run – to be the pillar and bulwark of the truth about him who was manifest in the flesh, who was seen by angels, who was preached in the world, who was believed by men and women, who was received up into glory.

Read 1 Timothy 4

A. ASCETIC HERESY – The flesh (1–5)
    1. Abstinence
        a. Source – deceiving spirits
        b. Substance – denying senses
    2. Acceptance
        a. Created by God
        b. Consecrated by gratitude

B. ATHLETIC HOLINESS – The faith (6–10)
    1. Teaching for goodness
    2. Training for godliness
    3. Toiling for God

C. APOSTOLIC HELP – The flock (11–16)
    1. Exhortation
    2. Example
    3. Exposition
    4. Exercise
    5. Experience
    6. Examination

I have mentioned my own studies in agriculture which were a very great help when I became a pastor. Moses studied agriculture under Jethro, his father-in-law. It was preparation for leading his people through the same place where he looked after sheep. David learnt about agriculture before he became a leader in Israel, and he was a shepherd. It is quite astonishing when you study the scriptures how many leaders of men had been leaders of animals first. Now that is not because people are like animals but because shepherding has similarities wherever you are, though my task as a shepherd in the hills of Northumberland was very different from the task of a shepherd in the hills of Judea. I can sum it up in two words. A shepherd in Judea has these main functions, which are listed in the 23rd Psalm: *provision* and *protection*. By provision I mean finding food for the animals. I sometimes had to do that in the winter. I remember helicopters coming and dropping hay during the snows of 1947. But normally you just let the sheep loose and there is green grass everywhere you look, or heather, or something for them to nibble at. But in the hills of Judea it is barren. A shepherd may have to take his flock fifteen miles to get food for them. He has to know when to make them lie down and rest and when to make them walk. He has to care for them until he can find them a bit of food, and then he makes them lie down in green pastures. But the other thing is that he constantly has to guard against wild beasts who will harm them. That is something I never had to do in Northumberland. I was not scared of lions appearing around the corner or wolves coming out of the bush. There used to be wolves in England. The last one was killed in some woods near Allendale, Northumberland. But we are not scared of them any more.

When Jesus preached the Sermon on the Mount he said, "Beware of wolves in sheep's clothing." I have never seen a wolf in sheep's clothing and I don't think there is a wolf intelligent enough to get hold of a fleece, pull it around his shoulders, then creep in among the flock. At this point both Jesus, and Paul after him, use a picture which is a metaphor that is mixed if you like – concerning something that could never happen to ordinary sheep but does happen to the sheep of Christ's flock. What do the "wolves" do, how do they do it, and why are people fooled? A wolf, according to Jesus and Paul, is a man who infiltrates a Christian church with false teaching. The tragedy is that he looks like a sheep, he looks like a Christian and he behaves like a Christian. If he came dressed as a wolf they would not look at him, but he is nice and kind and friendly and people are fooled. He subtly distorts the truth and that is the way the sheep of God are fed with poison.

A shepherd therefore has a double duty. Part of it is nice and part of it is not so nice. Here it is: as a shepherd I must see that the flock get the right food. That is a nice task, a holy privilege, because if you are teaching others you know far more yourself. A good teacher keeps one step ahead of his pupils – that is all. The other part of my task is not so nice – it is to tell you that today, as in every century, every day yet for two thousand years, there are nice, kind, friendly people inside the church who could fool you if you never asked them what they really believed. If you ask them you will be shattered and you will discover that they do not believe the Bible to be true. You will discover that they do not believe what you have always assumed they believe – and that is destructive. It will come out in a discussion group or in so many ways. It will come out in prayer, and it is subtle poison. Paul is concerned with this and he teaches Timothy that the Holy Spirit says expressly that there will come days when this kind of subtle perversion of teaching will creep in through people who are so nice that you could be fooled, and you can always test them by the Word of God. You must not test them by their appearance, you must not judge by the eyes, because the Lord never does.

Verses 1–5 are concerned with a particular heresy, which had already got into the church: Gnosticism. If you put a letter "a" in front of the word, it becomes *a*gnosticism, which we have to battle with today. There are even those within the church who claim to be Christian agnostics. That is like talking about a square circle. Jesus came to bring us the truth, and the truth sets us free, and we know whom we have believed – we are not agnostics. But in those days there were Christian Gnostics – which means the Christian know-alls.

Put simply, they were teaching that the physical and the spiritual can never meet – that the physical is evil and the spiritual is good, and that therefore you must keep these two things widely separated. You must not let your spiritual life interfere with your physical life, or your physical life interfere with your spiritual. That may be a strange belief to you but if you make for a Christian Science church you will hear it today, but you hear it from others too.

Funnily enough, it has two opposite extreme effects. If my spiritual life has nothing to do with my body but only my soul, I will do one of two things. I will either over-indulge my body and say, "It doesn't matter as long as I say my prayers, I can do what I like with my body." So it leads to an extreme immorality. Or it will go the other way and I will say, "If I'm to be a saint, I must do everything I can to get rid of my body and its appetites. I must sit on a bed of nails; I mustn't get married. I must stop eating this food and stop drinking that drink. I must mortify every desire of the body if I'm going to be free in spirit." Now these are two extreme views which you will find to this day in the church. On the one hand are those who say, "It doesn't matter what you do with your body. As long as you are a faithful pray-er, as long as you read your Bible, and as long as you go through all the other spiritual side, you are excused from behaving right with your body." It is astonishing how widespread that view is today and how big a gap is growing between religious, spiritual activity, and physical activity on the other hand, but the Bible keeps them together. Then there are those who have made laws and rules and sought an ascetic life which denies the things of the body as being good at all. In the matter of sex there are those who think that, provided they pray, witness and worship, they can do whatever they want. On the other hand are Christians who think that sex is in itself a dirty and sinful thing. More than once I have counselled Christian couples who had not achieved sexual compatibility in marriage because they had somehow been brought up with a guilt complex about the very act itself, because of the teaching and attitudes of the church. These extremes are due to the fact that the spiritual and the physical have not been kept together. "Glorify God in your body," says Paul. "Know you not that your body is the temple of the Holy Spirit?" Keep the spiritual and physical together.

Let us see what they were doing here. The particular heresy that Paul mentions is the ascetic kind that says if a thing is of the body it must be bad; if your body wants to do something, that must be sin. It is astonishing how many fall into this and the idea does not come from the human mind but from demonic spirits. The demons would love to get your ideas twisted. If they can get you separating life into a spiritual compartment and a physical compartment, and keep the two shut against each other, they have achieved something very mighty. Demonic spirits get hold of people and then sear their conscience, which means cauterise it – kill its nerves so that the conscience no longer acts in this matter, and then you can separate the two. They then began to deny the senses. For example, they forbade marriage. Again within the church, there has been for centuries an idea that celibacy is a more spiritual state than marriage. Paul did advocate celibacy for some. For certain kinds of Christian service a man without a wife and family is freer from responsibilities. Quite naturally, it is not easy for a man who, say, has to go out and spend hours with someone else helping them spiritually and then comes home and has his wife say, "Where have you been?" My wife doesn't. But it is not easy for a man who is trying to do Christian work to balance his responsibilities towards his family. We can't always spend as much time with our children as we would like. But Paul never advocated celibacy because sex was sinful, on the contrary he said the holiest things about Christian marriage and about physical union between a man and a woman. If anybody gets the idea that sex in itself is sinful then they have denied the truth of scripture: "And God said, 'Let us make man.' And he made man male and female and said, 'That's very good.'"

Or take food—these people were saying a Christian mustn't eat this and mustn't eat that. Vegetarianism is one example. A person who says every Christian ought to be a vegetarian hasn't read the Bible, where God not only tells us to eat the flesh of animals but deliberately says that Jesus did – and I follow Jesus. But I remember going to a house meeting once where our hostess was a real dab hand at cooking and she had made some cream cakes. (If the devil gets hold of me it will be through cream.) She brought in a tray of these beautiful cream cakes and they were almost too lovely to touch. We sat down and half-way through tea our host, a good Christian man, suddenly said, "I have just read in a Christian magazine that gluttony is the besetting sin of modern Christians." I had just taken one of those cakes in my hand. Well, having touched it I couldn't put it back obviously, it wouldn't have been polite, so I had to eat it. You know, most of those cream cakes went back into the kitchen. But we had started that by saying grace, saying thank you to God. If you are starting to say, "You must eat this and you mustn't eat that," you have fallen into this trap of asceticism.

Consider drink. Jesus drank fermented wine and so did the early Christians, or else they could never have been accused of getting drunk at communion. The early church had fermented wine at communion and this is quite clearly the position there. They were told to be moderate and temperate. We are never told not to drink because it is wrong in itself. But Paul does say (and it is why I am teetotal) that if I have a brother for whom I am responsible who cannot hold a drink and whose conscience is being hurt by it, then I must come off it – not because it is wrong, but because of Christian love for the other person. Paul says: "I will neither eat meat nor drink wine, if by doing that I am causing a weaker brother to stumble." So those who teach continuing abstinence are beginning to fall into this ascetic heresy. Paul teaches that if you can thank God for it because he created it, then it is right for you to have it. If you read 1 Corinthians 10, it is so clear there. All things are lawful to me, not all things are helpful. I can take anything that God has created, thank him for it and eat and drink. But it is not a *secular* activity. "Whether you eat or drink, do all to the glory of God."

I know there can be abuse and that you can become a glutton. I know that you can become a winebibber. I know that you can be become a libertine. But the basic desires of the body are good, and God made them, and they are to be received with thanksgiving and consecrated by the word of God and prayer. How difficult it is to walk a balanced way between doing everything as much as you want on the one hand and going around making laws for Christians that are not in the Bible on the other hand.

We move on to verses 6ff. I don't believe the world will ever be one family unless men come to have one Father, which they don't at the moment. But that is our task. In army training there are three stages to making a good soldier. Stage number one is *teaching*, which may be sitting in a room with an officer or NCO giving talks, lectures, telling him what to do. Second, *training* in which he learns to do it himself, in which he must take part in exercises, which may not be real. They may be dummy bullets, they may be blanks, but he has got to be trained in those conditions. Thirdly, there is the actual fighting in battle when it comes. Unless he has gone through the first two he will let the army down in stage three. I am not upholding war here, I am using an illustration which both Jesus and Paul did. But behind verses 6–10 is a picture of Greek gymnasia. They were great on physical training in those days. They had the Olympic games and other events, and everywhere you went in ancient Greece there were large stadiums for sport. They worshipped health and beauty. Indeed, you can see that if you go around the British Museum and look at the friezes and statues. The Greeks worshipped physical form and fitness. Between the ages of sixteen and eighteen every young man received physical education. The Greeks thought that a nation that was physically fit would be invincible. Now the associations were often with immorality and idolatry, even in the gymnasia – immorality, because they were always stark naked when they did their exercises; idolatry because the games were held in honour of their gods. The altars were lit when the games were held. That still survives in the Olympic Games. A runner comes in and lights the torch, and he is lighting it to the gods, so that the gods might be pleased with the smoke that ascends and the flame is on the altar of youth and sport.

Against that background, Paul is saying to Timothy that just as people train for sports you must train for spiritual fitness. He does not rule out the body. He says bodily exercise profits, but compared with spiritual exercise it profits little. He does not say that it doesn't profit at all. The three stages in spiritual fitness are teaching, training, and toiling for God. Teaching – to be told the right thing; training – to learn to do it; toiling – getting into the battlefield. Quite simply, you need to listen to someone teaching sound doctrine. Then you need to learn to practise that within the fellowship of the church, which is the easiest place to learn. Then you need to go out into the battlefield – maybe your home, your workplace, school or college – and there you need to toil and strive for God.

We can illustrate this even more directly. If you are ever going to be used as a witness to God, step number one is to listen to preachers and teachers. Step number two is to learn to talk about your faith to other Christians. If you cannot open your mouth in prayer and discussion among Christians, you will never open it in the world. If you can't talk about Jesus to those who love him, will you ever talk about him to anyone else?

Paul is teaching Timothy: If you put these instructions before the brethren.... There is an astonishing contrast sometimes between what people today call a good minister and what the Bible calls a good minister. A good minister is someone who will tell people these things: Timothy, you will be a good minister if you put these instructions before them and if you nourish yourself on the words of the faith and of good doctrine, and nourish them too. To study the Bible is like having a good meal. But you must have nothing to do with godless and silly myths. You must not just tell them religion and legends. Godless and silly myths are invented from the human mind. You tell them what I think

1 TIMOTHY 4

and you will be a good minister. Train yourself, and then you can train others. A minister has got to learn to practise what he preaches. This is where he has one tremendous advantage in being married and having a family, especially if they sit and listen to him. They make quite sure that he keeps up to what he says in the pulpit. "Remember what you said last Sunday...!" A preacher must train as well as teach, train himself and then others, and say: "Now you get into that group of Christians. You learn to pray. You learn to talk about Christ, learn to open your mouth. Learn to train. Bodily exercise is of some value, but spiritual exercise profits much." Some people spend a lot of time at a gym exercising, body building, and it profits, but it profits little – because all that time is being spent on what is for this world only.

Paul does not fall into the trap of the heretics who said the body is evil. The body is to be kept as fit as you can keep it for God's service, but the kind of training that Christians need to exercise themselves in is for eternity. When you train yourself to praise and to worship God you are training yourself for something you are going to do forever. Physical fitness will go, but godly exercise holds promise for the present life *and* the future.

Now let me underline this: If you just listen to Bible teaching and never learn to speak yourself, and never learn to pray out loud yourself, and never learn to talk to others about Christ, then quite frankly you will not be fit for the battle. You have missed out on essential training. Why do churches have house groups and other meetings? When you pray, when you take part, they are training you in godliness that you might be fit for the Master's use and ready for the battle. You never will be that if you're just a sermon taster, if you just come and listen—that's the first step.

Continuing the military metaphor: an army instructor might use diagrams and lectures to teach recruits how to fire a rifle, but then if he says, "Now go to war," even though the troops had never yet touched a gun or fired one, can you imagine what would happen? Well, the enemy pops up in front of the soldier and he runs for his book and says, "Now what page was it?" Then he finds the right page. Now he says, "What should I do?" By the time he has done that, he is dead. You see he has to translate the theoretical into the practical so his reactions will be instinctive. If you do not learn to speak about the things of Christ among other Christians I will tell you what will happen — when you are challenged about them in the world you will say, "Now, I'll have to ask my minister about that. Next week I'll try and get an answer for you." Have you had this experience? I learned in a fellowship of men to talk about my faith – among Christians. Then, when I was asked outside that setting, I was ready. I had already learned to do it in the right place – teaching, training, toiling. Hear about it from someone else, then practise it yourself, and then you can toil and strive for the battle.

There is an interesting and unusual phrase in v. 10, "For to this end we toil and strive." Why? Because, "... we have our hope set on the living God, who is the Saviour of all people, especially of those who believe." Does that mean God is going to save everyone? Or that everybody is a Christian? No, the word "Saviour" means "the preserver", and God is the preserver of all, or we would not be alive today. I believe that God stops wars at a certain point. He allows them to start, and he sets a limit for the simple reason that he has said that man will not destroy the world. I have no fears of a nuclear war that will end history. God has restrained us and preserves the human race. Thank him that he does. But those who believe, he keeps going in the next world too. So that is what is meant by this phrase, and because of this we toil and strive, and there is a battle that I have got to be fit for. We need to be taught and trained, and then go out and toil so that all men may become the special ones who believe and are saved for the next world. It may be that I am called to fight to save people's lives in this world, but God has called me to fight for people's freedom in the next, and to do that I must be as fit as any soldier in the army.

Therefore, finally, verses 11–16 are an exhortation to Timothy to be a good minister. Notice that he is exhorted to go on teaching and *command* these things. The preacher's job in the pulpit is not to say, "I venture to suggest..." but, "In the name of the Lord, I tell you." People may say that is narrow-minded, but Paul instructs Timothy: Command and teach these things, you have the authority of God behind you but you must be an example to the flock.

Timothy was a young man, under forty. Interestingly enough, they could be called into the army up to the age of forty. Paul's teaching is: don't let them look down on you because you are young. Timothy is to give an example in the very qualities that are normally lacking in youth: gravity, prudence, consideration, trustworthiness and mastery over passion. He must give himself to preaching, the public reading of scripture, and to teaching – the most important thing that a minister can ever do.

Timothy must study to show himself approved unto God; he must exercise the gifts that God had given him when he was ordained, when hands were laid on him for this ministry. He must have an experience that will grow, so people can say, "I can see that his experience is deeper now than it was five years ago." Finally, he must examine himself and his teaching so that he never puts himself in the position where neither he nor his hearers will get saved.

Will you train in godliness? Will you go to your next house group and will you pray there if you have never prayed there before? Will you make every opportunity you can to get into a smaller fellowship meeting where you can open your mouth and talk about things of the Lord? If you feel that a small meeting is too big then will you go to one Christian and talk to them about Christ and learn to pray with them? Will you please train and don't stop hearing teaching? The one horror I have in stirring up the gift that God gave me when I was ordained to the ministry, which was a gift of teaching, is of producing an audience rather than an army, of producing a bunch of sermon-tasters who are anxious to hear some new thing but who will not themselves train to do what God made me do. I beg you, therefore, to train, then toil and strive, for our hope is in the living God, who is the Saviour of all men, and especially of those who believe.

Read 1 Timothy 5

Introduction (1–2)
    fathers brothers mothers sisters

A. WIDOWS (3–16) – deacons' work
    1. Enriching their supplies (3–8)
        a. The church's duty
        b. The family's debt
        c. The widow's devotion
           i. Prayer!
           ii. Pleasure?
    2. Enrolling their services (9–16)
        a. Older
           i. Their desires – married once
           ii. Their duties – industrious
        b. Younger
           i. Their desires – marry again
           ii. Their duties – idle

B. WORKERS (17–20) – elders' work
    1. Rewarding their services (17–18)
        a. Their work
        b. Their wages
    2. Rebuking their sins (19–20)
        a. Witnesses in private
        b. Warning in public

Conclusion (21–25)
    inclinations impatience illness impressions

When you became a child of God you became part of a family. Chapter 5 has this theme: *our relationships with each other are to be those of a family.* We are going to live together in heaven, and we must learn to live together on earth. No Christian must run away from home.

How are we to regard each other within a family? When you meet an older man who is a Christian, talk to him as you would talk to your own father. When you meet a younger man who is a Christian talk to him as you would talk to your own brother. When you meet an older woman in the family of God, talk to her as if she were your mother. When you meet a younger woman in the family of God, talk to her as if she were your sister—that is verses one and two. If we always remembered that, then we would have far fewer problems. Under God the heavenly Father we are brothers, sisters, mothers and fathers, and there is no other way to behave in church.

Now two groups of special concern within the family are singled out. One is a group called the widows and the other I call the workers – the elders, the leaders who labour on behalf of the family. There is a great deal here about widows. There are three categories of women in the church, as in society: single women, married women and widows. Widows are in a category by themselves. They do not revert to being single, which is why our tradition is that a widow does not revert to her maiden name. She will be known by her married name for the rest of her life. A widow is in a very different situation from that of a single woman. God has a very special interest in the widow. This comes out in every part of the Word of God. If you read the Law of Moses or the Psalms, you will find again and again that

God is a father to the fatherless and a judge for the widow. The derivation of the word "widow" is "empty" or "void". When the earth was without form and void it was empty of life. It is interesting that this is the word used for those who have lost a husband, and God is especially concerned about them. They are under his special care and protection. In the Old Testament they received tithes and special offerings. He blesses all those who honour widows and he curses those who make their life more difficult by hurting them.

Widows are objects of Christ's special love. If you go through the four Gospels, particularly Luke, again and again you notice that he has a special eye for the widow. When the widow donates two small coins, the Lord's compassion goes straight out to her and he says, "Look, did you see what that woman did?" When he met a funeral procession of a widow with her only son being buried, he did something about it straightaway. When the Prince of life meets death, it is death that has to give way. Even when our Lord hung on the cross, in spite of his agony, the pain and the mocking, there was one concern he had for a widow, his own mother – to make provision and provide protection for her in the future. Almost his last act was to provide for his own widowed mother, so here we have a theme that runs right through the Bible. The very first deacons in the church were called together to look after this group. If you read Acts 6 you will find that deacons were first appointed because the widows were not being properly looked after. It should be a special concern of deacons still.

In New Testament days, unlike today, a widow would have no home, for the home passed on to the male side of the family. She would have no pension, no state assistance. Work would be hard to find. Few jobs were open to women in those days. Reading ancient history, if they were young enough they often resorted to immoral means of getting money just to stay alive. A widow in those days was very much worse off materially than one today. We need to remember that when we read these words.

Paul says to Timothy that widows are to be honoured. Unfortunately, that word has changed its meaning and it now means "to respect" or "to look up to". But in those days it meant something very much more practical – it meant to give them money, to support them. The word has become our word "honorarium". I think it would be much better if we translated the word "honour" in scripture with "honorarium" – except that is not a verb! But when it says "honour widows" it means "give them an honorarium", "support them financially." We have a duty to do this. Where a person has no other means of support, the church has a responsibility and a duty to support that person.

So Paul lays this on the church through Timothy – that is the church's duty. But lest sentiment take over and we do things we ought not to do, he immediately goes on to say that this only applies to someone who has no-one else to support them and no other means of support. If there are relatives, the church should not support someone, it is the duty of those relatives to do this. The church should not do things that excuse other people from their responsibilities.

It is interesting that, in the scriptures, orphans and widows are linked together as those who have no-one to help. James says, "Pure religion and undefiled before the Father is this, to visit the orphan and the widow in their affliction...." – giving is to go to those who have no-one else to help. Therefore we have a duty to ask, "Who are those within our circle, within our reach today, who have no-one else to help them?" These are the people to whom we should be going with very practical help. So relatives have a duty to God and a duty to a widow. It is their religious duty to look after such a person – it is a debt, to repay what they have received.

THE PERSONAL LETTERS

I remember sitting down with an old man on a park bench many years ago, in Newcastle on Tyne, just after I became a Christian. I started talking to him and asked him where he lived. He said, "In the workhouse over that railing." (He still called it that.) Now he was medically fit, he was mentally fit, he did not need care. Some do, and may need nursing, either physically or mentally, in their old age. He was quite fit but just old.

I said, "Have you no family?"

"Yes," he replied, "I have four sons, all married, all with good jobs, but they don't bother to come and see me now."

So there was a situation where a man with four married sons, all of them with means, was being just left alone. Now according to this chapter such a thing cannot happen among Christians. Here we have the Word of God on this very clearly indeed. There is a cynical old Dutch proverb that has an element of truth in it: "It seems easier for one poor father to provide for five children than for five rich children to provide for one poor father."

We come then to v. 8, which is as clear as anything you will ever read in the New Testament: "If anyone does not provide for his relatives, and especially for his own family, he has disowned the faith and is worse than an unbeliever." Could anything be clearer, stronger or more challenging than this? I am not giving you my opinion here, I am passing on to you the Word of God. One of the things about working through the Bible is that you come to texts like this, which I have never heard taken as a text for a sermon, but there it is. This chapter is not concerned with inspiration; it is not concerned with lifting you up to heavenly places – it is concerned with *instruction*, enabling you to live right, down here on earth. Some people want every time they come to church to be lifted up, thrilled and excited, then go home singing. There are times when, thank God, he does this for us. There are other times when God says, "Now you just go home and provide for your family. Go home and get a job and work and do what you should do." Not to provide is to be worse than an unbeliever. Why worse? Well, I will tell you why. First, because unbelievers do this anyway – they neglect their relatives. Second, they do not know the command of God. Third, they don't have the love of Christ or the Spirit of God to help them. Therefore, if I don't do what Gentiles don't do, I am worse than they are. I know, and I have the resources that they do not have.

This is very serious and it involves all of us and a lot of heart-searching. It faces us with responsibilities. The church has a duty to look after those whom no-one else will look after. I remember meeting an Arab Christian. Shortly after he had become a Christian he said, "My wife and I are going to turn our home into an orphanage." There were orphans on every street corner, begging in order to live. This was his instinctive response – his immediate outworking of salvation. Then he learnt of the story of that great saint George Muller, and said, "He did the same."

Now to the duty of relatives. If the person in need has relatives, then it is their responsibility before God to help, not to impose that need on the church, so that the church is free to help others. Verse 16 says: "If any believing woman has relatives who are widows, let her assist them and let the church not be burdened, so that it may assist those who are real widows." In one church in which I was minister, we opened a home for old people, which later had about twenty-two elderly residents and then an extension was started for another twelve people. It was a wonderful work of grace, and the Lord provided every penny that was needed. But our main problem in the early days was selecting residents – those who really were in need and whom no-one else could look after. We were approached by many families who simply wanted somewhere to put old dad, just like that. So we had to pray and be very careful, selecting those who were in real need, in order that the church should not be burdened by those who were not.

We have now learnt about the church's debt or duty and the family's debt, now we are also told about the widow's obligations. For the widow who is being looked after by the church also has an obligation: in gratitude for the help the church gives, to give herself to prayer; to do the one thing she can do to help the church to be what it ought to be. I thank God for widows and elderly people who give themselves to prayer – they are doing as much for the church and for the world as anyone I know. I was deeply moved when I got a letter one week from a dear old lady in a Leicester old people's home. She said, "I've never met you and probably never will. But I want you to know that I pray every day for your ministry." To think that I can get up in the morning and know that old lady is praying "Lord, help him" is a tremendous inspiration. So if somebody is being supported by the church, there is a way in which they can repay that by praying. The tragedy is that many people reach old age and cannot exercise a ministry of spiritual support because they have never developed that ministry through their life. So bingo rather than the Bible fills out the long, dreary hours! When an old person has the time to sit quietly and pray around the church and support the pastor, the deacons and the members – what a ministry!

So Paul says, "Let them give themselves in supplication and prayer night and day," because many old folk don't sleep very well. One of the ways they can redeem the night hours when they lie awake is just to go around the church and think of people and pray for them. They are doing more than perhaps most of us who rush around pretending to be so busy. They are at the throne of grace, pouring their supplication into the church and carrying the others.

The alternative is rather stark: "Whereas she who is self-indulgent is dead even while she lives" (v. 6). I am afraid the phrase "merry widow" is proverbial. What Paul is really meaning here is that a widow who is being supported must not therefore spend her time enjoying herself but must give herself to a ministry of prayer and supporting others. Otherwise she is dead while she is alive. Somebody said to me about one person, "They were dead at fifty, though they weren't buried till they were seventy." What a comment on a life! Whereas those who instead of giving themselves to enjoying themselves give themselves to a ministry are spiritually alive – you meet them; you go to them. I think of an elderly lady, in her eighties. She gave herself to this ministry, and teenagers used to flock to her little flat. Some people would have said, "She's right out of their bracket, look how she dresses; nobody would be interested in her if they were young." But they would have been wrong. You see, she was praying for those young people in their jobs. She was praying for them while they studied. They knew it. She was very much alive.

In vv. 9–16, Paul talks about the enrolling or enlisting of widows, older ladies supported by the church. Now what does he mean by "enrolled"? The answer is: to be enrolled in the service of the church as deaconesses, to serve the members in practical ways. We know from other writings that the early church had a list of enrolled widows who, having looked after their own home and family, were called by the church to go into other homes and help others. The qualifications are severe: they are to have been married once and then a list of most lovely things is found. They are to have brought up children so they can counsel young mothers. They are to have shown hospitality, so that they can use a home unselfishly. They are to have washed the feet of saints, which means they are to be the sort of people who would not count any task for another too dirty or too menial. They are to have relieved the afflicted – which means this is the sort of person who has spotted a need and has done something about it; and they are to have been devoted to doing good. It leads me to think of Proverbs 31, that chapter about an ideal wife, which is a beautiful picture of an ideal household manageress. Wives read it, but husbands please leave it strictly alone. It is for your wives that it was written But in the early church a woman who had been a good housekeeper, a good mother, a good neighbour – when the church took her into their support they would say: we want you now to regard the church as your family, and we want you to go around and help people from house to house. We want you to be free to do this, and we enrol you as a deaconess. They were only enrolled if they were over sixty years of age because the possibility was that if they were younger they would remarry. So this was in a sense a pledge to marry the church. In later centuries some women took vows to remain unmarried for the sake of the church, and so orders of nuns were established. But in the New Testament a deaconess was a lady who gave herself to the church and for that reason pledged herself not to marry. A younger widow would find that more difficult for two reasons. First, she might find herself wanting a home and family of her own again. This is being sensitive and understanding. Who says that Paul didn't understand women? Don't you believe it, he did. He knew that a single woman and a widow may be in two very different positions. One has had desires and affections aroused which the other has not. Therefore, he said that a younger widow is better to marry again and have again the home life that she had before, and it would be wrong to ask them to pledge their troth, as a deaconess, to Christ, not to marry but to be the housekeeper of the church. So the younger widows were told not to consider this. The other reason was that the temptation might be instead of going round other homes to provide help, rather to go around to talk. Deaconesses are not to go around to talk, they are to go around to help – to help young mothers to manage their children, to help people to cook, to assist people to do things that are helpful—that is what a deaconess is for, not to talk, talk, talk. The danger is that if they talk they become not busy workers but busybodies. Paul has a lovely play on the Greek words there, making a pun.

All this is terribly practical. Lest I be shot down in flames for saying that women are gossips, in another epistle Paul applies the words "gossips" and "busybodies" to men. So he understood men too.

We turn from this important matter of the widows, which to us means anyone who has no-one to look after them. We should support them, and if possible we should enrol them for the service of the church so that they can support the family. We now come to the workers, the elders, those men who are called by the church to rule. Let me remind you that it is God's pattern of organising the church to have a group of men in it who rule together and who govern the family. We are told that they should be honoured. Once again, the modern English completely disguises what the Bible says. I am so glad the NEB actually rendered it correctly: "Let the elders who rule well be considered worthy of double stipend". It immediately goes on to say "the labourer deserves his wages," which could hardly be clearer. In other words, the pattern in the early church was supported widows going around from home to home helping people in a practical way with their families and so on, and supported elders. Quite frankly, one of the problems today is that I hardly know of a man who has time to be an elder – gifts, yes, but not the time. The early church found that the time needed for elders to help to rule the flock demanded they be supported financially, which by clear implication means that a man with a full-time job really has not time to be an elder.

So they had a full-time ministry of women to help practically, and of men to lead spiritually. So there was a double honour for those who did their work well, which quite frankly means a financial bonus, even in spiritual service. That is a scriptural way of looking at things. Especially those who labour in preaching and teaching – which takes even more time than looking after people. So the principle is laid down: "You mustn't muzzle the ox when it is treading out the grain," which likens elders to oxen. We will accept that. The word of our Lord is then quoted: "The labourer is worthy of his wages." Timothy has been warned not to be a money-grabber, and a man who is in Christian service for the money is a man who ought not to be in Christian service. But you don't need to keep your elders poor to keep them pure. So this is clear teaching.

We come to something else in vv. 19–20. Elders are human and can go wrong and because they are in the public eye and because they lead, they are subject to criticism. Because they exercise discipline over others this can be resented, and then criticisms can be made. How do you deal with such criticism? Firstly, you never listen to criticism of an elder unless it comes from two or three independent witnesses. Churches should remember that little rule. Secondly, when they have come, you tell him privately. You do not tell anyone else. Thirdly, if he then puts it right, nothing more is said. But if he persists in wrongdoing then you should say something publicly in front of the church, that all may fear. Now there is clear guidance for today. If there is something wrong with the leaders of the church, make sure it is from two or three witnesses. Go and see them privately, rebuke them privately, and if they put it right that is an end to it. If they don't, then and only then should it come to the church.

Finally, Timothy is told a number of little potted bits of advice as a minister, to be practical. He is warned not to have favourites, to do nothing from partiality – a very important point. He is told not to be impatient in laying on of hands, meaning don't choose elders quickly. It takes a lot of time, a lot of prayer and a lot of thought to choose an elder. Otherwise you participate in his sins. Verse 23: a pastor should look after his health, if necessary by ceasing to be a total abstainer. Because of the water in those days you can understand why. He was obviously subject to dysentery, which was affecting his ministry – take a little wine for the sake of your stomach. He didn't mean him to rub it in! I am sure he meant him to drink it.

Finally, v. 24: don't go by first impressions of people. That is a very important word to a minister, especially when he goes to a new pastorate. What Paul is teaching here is: Timothy, bad points may take some time to come out; good points may take some time to come out. Just be patient and wait until you really know a person before you rush in and say, "You be an elder" or some other office holder.

All this may not make you shout "Hallelujah!" but if it helps churches to live as families, to have right relationships with each other, and particularly with two groups of people – those who have no-one else to help them and those who rule over us in the church – then it has been a worthwhile study.

Read 1 Timothy 6

A. WORK – CONSCIENTIOUS (1–2)
    1. Godless master
    2. Godly master

B. WORDS – CONSTRUCTIVE (3–5)
    1. Conceited
    2. Contentious
    3. Covetous

C. WEALTH – CONTENTED (6–10)
    1. Death of the body
    2. Desire of the mind
    3. Destination of the soul

D. WALK – CONSTANT (11–16)
    1. Aim of the Christian
        a. Flee
        b. Follow
        c. Fight
    2. Appearing of the Christ

E. WEALTH – CONSIDERED (17–19)
    1. Deception
        a. Superiority
        b. Security
    2. Distribution
        a. Goodness
        b. Generosity

F. WORDS – CONSISTENT ((20–21)
    1. Deposit of truth
    2. Danger of talk

When you first read a chapter of the Bible, one of the most helpful things is to take out a pen and underline any word that occurs quite frequently in the passage. I do hope you read your Bible with a pen. Don't mind if you make a mess of it, you can always buy another one if it is just too messed up to read. It is so helpful to underline things that are important. If you see two texts that seem to link up with each other, then draw a line linking them and you begin to see what God is saying.

When I first read 1 Timothy 6, one word jumped out of the page. It comes again and again in this chapter. Did you spot it? It is the word "godliness". There it is in verses 3, 5, 6 and 11. You never hear it except among God's people. The world might talk about greatness or goodness, but someone is actually great if they are godly, which means simply: you can look at their life and say, "I understand a little more of what God must be like by looking at that person." That is the aim and object of the Christian life: to be godly; to live a godly life in Christ Jesus.

We are now going to ask what godliness is. The opposite question would be, "What is worldliness?" Again you won't find the world using that word. The Christian is in the tension between worldliness and godliness – called to leave worldliness behind and to have godliness, not to be like everybody else but to be like our heavenly Father. Nothing could be simpler. But having said that, some people have a picture of godliness which is kind of heavenly other-worldliness that does not somehow resonate here. The godliness of which Paul is writing in this chapter is a godliness that shows in the office, in your bank account, in the kitchen, in fact wherever you are, because real godliness is related to the realities of life. It is concerned with everyday living. Even the first two verses might tell us enough to seek to live a godly life this week.

In the days when this was written, two out of every three people were slaves. They had come to be slaves in one of a number of ways. A prisoner captured in war was made a slave; a criminal might be bought out of prison as a slave; someone in debt might sell himself as a slave to pay his debts; someone could be kidnapped, taken somewhere else and then sold as a slave. Some could be simply sold by parents as a slave. That went on in the ancient world – a terrible practice – especially with girls. Finally, a person could be born a slave. If your father and mother were slaves that was it, you were born in chains. There were sixty million slaves in the Roman Empire, and some were treated terribly. They were whipped, they were branded, especially if they ran away, when they were branded with the letter "F" on their face – signifying the Latin word translated as "fugitive". They were branded so that they were marked for life. They were often crucified by their owners for displeasing service. You may be surprised to learn that most of the butchers in the Roman Empire were slaves, as were many bakers and most of the doctors.

In the early church in the time of which we are thinking, the majority of the members were slaves. A major group of people who responded to Christ were the slaves. I think of the period of slavery in America. In the Southern States there was a time when the one thing that made life bearable for the slaves was to sing, "When I get to heaven, gonna put on my shoes." They never wore shoes. They could sing about crowns and robes, and if you study the songs called "spirituals" from that era in parts of America, you catch something of the life, the hope and the joy of the early church. Of course the Communist would cynically say that religion was used to keep the slaves happy. Well, the real question is not whether it was used to keep them happy, but whether they were happy for a sound reason. The sound reason was that, even though their bodies were in chains, their souls were free, and they knew that one day they would be in glory with the Lord.

The attitude of the early church to slavery is relevant to the church's attitude today towards any exploitation of human beings and denial of civil rights. We have enough guidance in scripture to know what we ought to do about these things. The one thing we ought not to do, quite clearly, is to foment armed rebellion against the system. That will leave in its trail far worse things. Those who live by the sword will die by it, in this sense. What did the early church do about slavery? Did they encourage slaves to fight for their freedom? No, they sent the slaves back into the system with a new attitude. That is what ultimately smashed slavery, although it took many centuries and still has not disappeared from the world. In other words, the thing that will break inhuman exploitation is to send into that situation people with the mind of Christ, even among the exploited, even among those who are downtrodden. That is the Christian way to deal with it. When a runaway slave found his way to Rome (and many of them went there because it was the big city where you could hide), Paul got hold of him and said, in effect: I am going to send you back into slavery now that you are a Christian. I will write a letter to your owner, and I want you to be a good slave now.

The first two verses here tell slaves to be good slaves. That does not support slavery as a system – it tells a Christian slave that he is to be a good slave. Now this is one of the hardest parts of Christian ethics to practise. I am going to apply this to modern situations. None of us is a slave. Even though employers cannot buy and sell us, and we can now go to an employment tribunal about any injustice, many of us are in a relationship of employer/employee. Now what does this tell you? "Let all who are under the yoke of slavery regard their masters as worthy of all honour." There is not a word here as to whether the master is a good one or a bad one, kind or unkind. He is a master, and the right Christian attitude is to give him honour and respect whatever he is like.

I have known situations where a really difficult or bad boss was changed because one person in his employment gave him honour, and whereas all others gave him disrespect, a Christian broke through at a real level that changed his attitude. This is what the slaves were to do, and it is what we are to do. Your boss may not be a Christian; he may be a sinner bound for hell; he may be a difficult sort of irritating, unkind fellow; the Christian attitude is to give him honour. Why? Is it for his sake? No. Is it for your sake, so that it will make things easier for you? No. For only one reason: that the name of God is at stake. If you are known as a Christian and you show disrespect where honour is due, then it is the name of God that will suffer.

Now that is a situation where your boss is not a Christian, and where he may not deserve respect. But now we turn to verse 2: those who have believing masters. Frankly, this is even more difficult. Supposing your boss is a Christian, supposing he goes to church, supposing he even goes to the same church, it is not going to be easy to have the right relationship to him. It is very easy for a Christian employee to think that because their employer is Christian they can somehow presume upon that and have a relationship of undue familiarity – that is not true. We are told here in the scripture that we must not be disrespectful on the ground that they are members of the same church, or fellow Christians, or anything else. What a delicate balance there is here, and how difficult it is to have a right relationship to an employer, whether he or she be a sinner bound for hell or a saint bound for heaven. Let there be honour and respect. Indeed, if you have a Christian master you should give him exceptional service; you should not trade on the fact that because he is a Christian he won't sack you if your work is not done too well, and that because he is a Christian he should overlook and forgive every one of your little shortcomings. One should almost beware of being offered a job where there are only Christians working. Believe me it is one of the most difficult situations to get relationships right. I have met people who did this. A girl secretary was converted and, alas, she was the only Christian in the office when she was converted. I say "alas" because she left it just a few months later and came to me and said, "Isn't it marvellous? I've got a job in a Christian firm where everybody in the office is Christian." She thought she had stepped out of Egypt into Canaan. She is now back in a secular office, if that is the right phrase to use, and it is a pity she ever removed her witness from a place where she could have been the salt of the earth into a place where she found relationships very difficult indeed. For put a bunch of Christians together in an office and it is very hard to keep the same efficiency, the same business, the same relationships that ought to apply in an efficient workplace. There should be exceptional service when you are working for a believer.

We move on to v. 3. In the ancient Greek world, the entertainers of the time were not the pop singers they were the travelling lecturers. Anybody who had a nice line in lecturing or some novel philosophy could travel around and make a lot of money just by entertaining people with words. The Greeks were intoxicated with the exuberance of their verbosity. Sadly, it was possible for this attitude to creep into the church, as it is possible for anything to creep from world to church. The early church developed a lot of travelling speakers who went around with some new thing to say. Paul wrote about these people. He was warning Timothy to watch anybody who doesn't come with the kind of sound words that he had given. If someone were to come with different teaching that might be very interesting and novel, then they were not to be followed. Timothy is to give the teaching which accords with godliness, teaching that helps people to live right, and worship that will bring them close to God.

Three points are made concerning those who bring those new ideas about doctrine and morality. First of all, they are conceited, puffed up, yet they know nothing. Secondly, they are contentious – they love controversy. They can develop a taste for sharpening their wits on other people's minds. It was said of three well-known preachers in London some years ago that "one loved the Lord, one loved people and one loved an argument." It was one of the three who said that, so I am quoting him.

This is to be the important thing: we are to love the Word of God and love the teaching. Call us old-fashioned if you like; let people say that we are still stuck with something two thousand years old. Yes we are! We do not believe in new views. We believe in the old, old story. It is a very old story and it will always be old, and for that reason it will always be new. Contentious people produce envy, dissension, slander, suspicion, wrangling. What a list, a dreadful crop, an ugly harvest. Not only are they conceited and contentious, but they soon become covetous.

Why do they do it? One of the motives in the ancient world was sheer greed. It became not a calling but a career, not a means of helping others but a means of public gain rather than private service. That is a little bit of advice on godliness for those who are in teaching.

Now we come from the means of gain in v. 5 to the great gain of v. 6. Here again, we see practical godliness. I have now spent many years visiting godly people, and it is one of the greatest privileges of my life, for which I constantly thank God. I realise that many people don't have the privilege to the degree that I have it. The thing is that I have never yet met a godly person who was not really content. A really godly person is a really content person. I have been to see godly people in some of the poorest homes in England and some of the richest homes, and it doesn't follow that riches or poverty make for godliness, but a godly person is content.

In Philippians 4 Paul says, "I have learned in all things to be content, to have nothing and to have all things." Which do you think is the most difficult – to be content with nothing or to be content with everything? I wonder. I would guess from my experience that it is more difficult to be content with a lot than with a little. There is something about getting more that makes you want more. To be content with a lot is as much a triumph, if not more of the grace of God, as to be content with little. Paul says, "I can have all things, I can have nothing, and I'm content." Here he is telling Timothy: If you've got enough to eat and enough to wear, isn't that sufficient? After all, that will keep you going. If you have sustenance and warmth for the body, should you not be content? Why grasp? Why want this, that and the other? Why open your soul to the pressures of advertising? "Millions of others have something, so why shouldn't you?" We should be content if we have enough for physical life so that we can do the job that God has given us to do.

Paul now mentions three things which should remind us what a great gain contentment is. First of all, Paul reminds Timothy about *the death of the body*. You may have heard the proverb "a shroud has no pocket". Two women on a bus were discussing a very wealthy man who had died. One said, "How much did he leave?" The other said, "Everything" – which is exactly how much you will leave and exactly how much I will leave. We shall leave it all behind. You can't take it with you, therefore contentment is great gain because you are not going to fasten your life to things that you have to leave behind. "Where your treasure is, there your heart will be also." So the death of the body comes into this.

Secondly: *the desire of the mind*. A Greek philosopher Epicurus (who was not a Christian) said that the secret of contentment is not to add to a man's possession but to take away from his desires. That is a wonderful statement and the Bible would back that up. A content person is a person who is not always wanting. There is one exception to this, one thing a Christian covets and presses on to get, but it is something he can take with him beyond the grave.

Thirdly: *the destruction of the soul*. Not only does the death of the body tell you how foolish it is to want more and more, not only does the desire of the mind tell you this, but in fact, the destruction of the soul is also a factor that you must take into account. "Money is the root of all evil" is not a phrase you will find in the Bible. In v. 10 it is the *love* of money. Money can be a root of all kinds of good. Think what wonderful things money can do in service for the Lord. Money can save life; money can feed the hungry, provide clean water, clothe the naked and give shelter to those who haven't got a roof over their heads. Money isn't the root of any kind of evil. It was originally invented as something helpful, to avoid the system we call "barter", which was a clumsy means of exchange. Modern currency is just a piece of paper (or a digital unit) that can be used for many purposes, some of them good.

So money is not the root of all kinds of evil, but the love of it is. Because when a person comes to love it for its own sake, not for what it will do but just to have it, then I am afraid something has happened to him or her. He will become possessed by his possessions. You cannot be a slave of God and money; you cannot be possessed by both. It is a very sad case when someone is possessed by their possessions. They are not worth anything any more.

I remember seeing a notice outside a church, which said: "If you lost all your money, how much would you be worth?" That is a wonderful question. Here is a line from John Bunyan: "I am content with what I have, little be it or much, and Lord contentment still I crave because thou savest such."

In v. 11 we move on to the Christian's walk and we see the contrast in what a Christian is aiming at. Is it to build up his business to get more money? No. "As for you, man of God, shun all this." The secret of the Christian aim is in three words: flee, follow, fight. There are things we have to run away from, things that will catch us unless we flee. Shun all this, flee these things, don't let them catch up with you, avoid them at all cost. We are to follow what? Righteousness, godliness, faith, love, steadfastness, gentleness. Show me someone with those six things and I will show you a man or woman of God. But it is not a picnic, it is a fight. You will have to fight the good fight. What is this fight we have got to fight? It is the good fight of *the faith*. A Christian will have to hold on to the faith and fight for it. It is not pleasant fighting – you will have to oppose people who would deny the faith and those who water it down.

Flee this, follow that, and fight for the other. These are the three aspects of a man of God, who will do all three. Paul is instructing Timothy: you are used to fighting the good fight; you will stand alone, I know; you have made the good confession in front of many witnesses as Jesus stood alone before Pontius Pilate and stuck to the truth. You may have to stand all alone and say, "This is the faith," but go on fighting as a man of God should.

At this point Paul takes off in his language. He can't help

it. He writes, "Timothy I charge you, hold on to this until the appearing of the Lord Jesus," and then he just lets go, "King of kings, Lord of lords," and the language pours out, "the Blessed and only Sovereign, who alone has immortality and dwells in unapproachable light, whom no man has ever seen or can see, to him be honour and eternal dominion." Why does Paul take off like this? Because a man of God has his eyes fixed on this immortal God. When everybody else around him may be fighting against the faith, when everyone else around may be grasping for money, the man of God says: This invisible, immortal God, he's the one before whom I have to appear, I am answerable to him, I am responsible to him, and I must be what he wants me to be. Whatever the scholars say, whatever the worldly businessmen say, it's God I've got to answer to and one day I shall appear when he appears – "King of kings, Lord of lords." Wherever a man or woman of God may be, we are on his majesty's service.

Do you know you ought to have the bearing of a royal ambassador? An ambassador has dignity, honour and respect for the king who sent him to be an ambassador. A former British ambassador to Russia said: "The greatest temptation of an ambassador is to conform to the country in which he lives, but he must remain true to the country from which he comes." He pointed out that the embassy, in a sense, must be kept in the traditions of the country from which he came. It represents another land. He must remain British wherever he is and live in a British way. He is there to represent Britain. He must respect and honour the people to whom he speaks, and as an ambassador, in a sense, he has a peculiar relationship to the country in which he lives. Nevertheless, he has also diplomatic immunity. His orders come from his home sovereign. Now this is what we are – ambassadors for Christ. We are a colony of heaven. We live down here, but we are not going to let the world set the tone of our life.

1 TIMOTHY 6

We appear before the King of kings and Lord of lords. We come back at the end of our term of ambassadorship and then we say, "Lord, here is my service. I've tried to be your ambassador." The humblest office employee or the man cleaning the streets can do so as an ambassador for the King of kings and Lord of lords. The appearing of Christ is what should keep us in the centre of godliness.

Finally, Paul comes back again to wealth, with a particular word for Christians who become wealthy. You see, godliness keeps coming back to earth from heaven. Remember that, according to Christ's standards, most of us in the developed world are rich. There are two things we are not to be. We must not get a false idea of *superiority*, nor a false idea of *security*. Having a bigger bank balance does not make people any better than anyone else. "Tell them not to put their trust in riches." They can buy themselves out of certain situations, but let them set their hope on God, who richly furnishes us with everything to enjoy.

I remember the story of a rich man who had a large estate and one day, when walking around the grounds, he saw an artist painting. The wealthy man said to him, "Everything that you are painting in that picture is mine."

The artist replied, "But the beauty is mine."

God has richly given us all things to enjoy, and the meek shall inherit the earth. We do not need to have it all to enjoy it. He has given us all things richly to *enjoy*. We are going to inherit the lot because we are his children and joint heirs with Christ. You can look at anything that God has created and say, "I'm going to inherit that. I'll enjoy it now but I don't need to possess it." All things are yours in Christ.

So we shouldn't have superiority, we shouldn't have security. What should we have? We should have *goodness* and *generosity*. We should learn to give; learn to spend that money on other people; to be rich in good deeds, liberal and generous, laying up for ourselves a foundation for the future so that we may take hold of the life that is life indeed.

What are people really doing when they are buying things? They are trying to live. They are trying to find life, and they think that if they can get this, that and the other they can live; they can have life. Ah, but here Paul is saying this: If you will use your money to help others, the money that you don't need for food and clothing and the other practical needs of life, if you will use this for others, then you are taking hold of the life that is life indeed. A Christian once said in his testimony: "What I kept I lost, what I gave I have."

Finally, Paul comes back again to Timothy's *words*. Timothy, you have been entrusted with something very precious. Guard it. Don't listen," and this is quite literally, "avoid the godless chatter and contradictions of what is falsely called 'knowledge'" [or, literally, "scholarship"]. "Don't listen to the godless chatter of scholars. Guard what is entrusted to you. Hold it fast.

People will claim to have superior knowledge and say, "Well, we don't believe that nowadays. We have grown out of this; it's old fashioned."

Some have missed the mark as regards the faith. They have become terribly well educated, very intellectual, but they have lost the simple faith of the man of God.

"Grace be with you."

What a letter – it started with God and finishes with godliness.

Read 2 Timothy 1:1–2:13

A. PAST – POWER OF A SOUND MIND (3–10)
   1. Their separate calling (3–7)
      a. Paul
         i. His appointment ii. His ancestry
      b. Timothy
         i. His anguish ii. His ancestry iii. His anointing
   2. Their shared concern (8–10)
      a. Their duty
      b. Their doctrine

B. PRESENT – PATTERN OF A SOUND MESSAGE (11–18)
   1. Their separate exercise (11–14)
      a. Paul
         i. Appointed ii. Suffering iii. Confident
      b. Timothy
         i. Follow ii. Guard iii. Entrust
   2. Their shared experience (15–18)
      a. Desertion
      b. Devotion

C. FUTURE – PROMISE OF A SOUND MASTER (1–13)
   1. Their separate functions (1–10)
      a. Timothy
         i. Soldier ii. Athlete iii. Farmer
      b. Paul
         i. Prisoner ii. Preacher
   2. Their shared future
      a. Vindication
      b. Victory

When a man comes to the end of his earthly pilgrimage, he doesn't waste time talking about the weather! We have now come to the last letter which Paul ever wrote – and he knew that it would be. Here is an older man writing to a young man and giving him a final word of advice. You can see from this letter the deep personal relationship that existed between Paul and Timothy – "my beloved child".

As far as we know Paul was never married, but he had many "children". He was a spiritual father to people all over the Roman Empire ("Timothy, I remember you constantly"), and like a good old man Paul turns his memories into prayers: "I remember you constantly in prayer"; "I remember your tears". What tears? When did Timothy cry? Surely when Paul was arrested for the last time – because the first letter was written while Paul was free to travel, but this final letter is written by an old man in fetters, lying in some room in the metropolis of Rome. "I remember your tears and I long to see you so that I may be filled with joy." Paul is also going to recall that moment when he himself laid his hands on the head of the young man and prayed and something happened.

Let us look first for the keywords in this passage which jump out of the page. There are three. The first is the word *gospel* which occurs five times. This gives you the clue to Paul. Here was a man who did not live for money or for his career, his hobby or sport; here was a man who lived for the gospel, and it was his sole ambition to spread it, to preach it. His whole life since his conversion has centred around this one thing: the gospel.

The next keyword in this section is *suffering*, which occurs four times, always in connection with the gospel. In v. 8 "Take your share of suffering for the gospel"; in v. 11,

"For this gospel I was appointed, and therefore I suffer as I do"; In 2:9, "The gospel for which I am suffering". If you live for the gospel, you are going to suffer. Christ did not promise us a cushion but a cross. Indeed, in chapter 3 it says quite plainly: "All who desire to live a godly life in Christ Jesus will be persecuted." So if you don't want to suffer, don't live for the gospel, but if you are going to live for the gospel, expect to suffer.

Another word that comes only three times but is obviously a keyword is *ashamed* – in connection with suffering for the gospel. Again, in v.8, "Do not be ashamed but take your share of suffering for the gospel"; also v. 11. In v. 16 too, about Onesiphorus, who was not ashamed. Because the gospel brings suffering, our temptation is to be ashamed of it. When we live for the gospel we become unpopular, people laugh at us and make our lives uncomfortable. Timothy was timid, and this shy, rather reserved, delicate young man was tempted to be ashamed because he had to suffer for the gospel. Paul is writing this whole section to build up Timothy so that he will not be ashamed to acknowledge the gospel but will be ready to take his share of suffering.

If you find at work or among your neighbours that you are ashamed to acknowledge that you are a Christian, that you are embarrassed to tell them that you go to church, that you are ashamed because you would not like the various little social handicaps that come to someone who stands for the gospel, then read this chapter. Three things will build you up. One concerns Timothy's past, one his present, and one his future. Paul goes through these three things and is saying: Timothy, look back into the past for a moment and remember that you were endowed by God with the power of a sound *mind*. We will see what that means in a moment. Then secondly: Look into the present Timothy – you have been entrusted with the pattern of a sound *message*. Now

Timothy, thirdly look into the future. You have been enlisted, called up, conscripted, with the promise of a sound *master*, who if you have to suffer will most certainly reward you.

Whenever you are tempted to be ashamed of the gospel and a little embarrassed to speak openly of the Lord, then remember those three things for they apply to you too.

One of the keys to understanding what Paul means here is to look at the personal pronouns – I, you, we, them, us, he – and begin to notice how they occur. You notice that under each heading, the past, the present and the future, Paul first of all deals very personally with himself and Timothy, "I and you"; "you and I". Then, after he has dealt particularly with Timothy, he deals with some general truth that applies to others and will use a general term like "us", "them" or "we", so that under each section he deals with himself and Timothy, and then generally with all Christians. It is particularly those general passages that concern us. For example, I didn't have a mother called Eunice and I didn't have a grandmother called Lois. That obviously is personal to Paul and Timothy. But the very next verse, "For God did not give us a spirit of timidity but a spirit of power and love and of self-control" does apply to me – I am in that. Likewise, in the next section Paul writes, "I suffer as I do". Well, I am not suffering as he did so that verse does not apply to me. But when he refers to a general description of those who are suffering for the Lord, that does apply. He is addressing Timothy and himself. He writes about "the fetters I am wearing". You have probably never had to wear chains for the gospel. But when he becomes general and says, "If we endure we shall reign with him" that does apply to me. I am in the "we". If I endure what I have to suffer then I shall reign with Christ just as Paul does, just as Timothy will.

Now look at vv. 3–10. This concerns the past. It is looking back all the time – an old man and his memories. Have you noticed that the older you get the more you live in the past? This is natural and not a bad thing. You will find that an old man will say "I remember" – and off he goes. He pours out his memories, "Ah that reminds me..." and out it comes. Of course the younger generation who did not live in those days often find this boring.

Paul has been on the road as a missionary for a long time. He has been imprisoned, beaten – he has been through it for thirty years. I don't know how old he was when he was converted, maybe about thirty, which would put him in his sixties, and we have, in vv. 3 and 4, "I remember"; v. 5, "I'm reminded" and v. 6, "I remind you". The word "remember" here concerns something remembered all the time, but to be reminded is something that just occurs to you. Here are two sorts of memory: the things you can never forget and the things that suddenly come back to you. So Paul is explaining: I remember you all the time. Every day he prays for Timothy, whose grandmother and mother he can remember well. Let us look back at what Paul is remembering. First: Timothy's anguish (v. 4). He says, "I remember your tears." It must have been a very sad moment when Timothy said goodbye to Paul, when the Roman soldiers led Paul away and Timothy thought he would never see the apostle again.

There are people who don't like Paul – especially some ladies – feeling that he is a very hard, tough man, not likeable. So may I remind you that whenever we are told he had to leave people, they cried. When he left the elders at Ephesus they wept because they would see his face no more. Why? Because he was a man who had dealt faithfully with them. He said, "I declared the whole counsel of God to you." He did not just give them the nice bits, he gave them the whole truth. Timothy was sorry to say goodbye to his spiritual father.

Secondly, Paul, looking back, remembers Timothy's ancestry. What a privilege it is to have had godly parents or grandparents. Paul remembered that Timothy had a mother who was a Jewish believer. The important thing is that my grandmother may have had faith and my mother may have had faith, but that does not mean that I have. There comes a day when I deliberately choose to have the Saviour my parents or my grandparents had. Then, as Paul says of Timothy: "Now I am sure the same faith that they had dwells in you."

Do you notice that in v. 3 Paul remembers his fathers (ancestors) but in v. 5 he remembers Timothy's mother and grandmother? Timothy did not have anything from his father's side, and this is so in many homes today. There are situations where a mother has a faith that might bring the child through to know the Lord, but the father hasn't. How much we owe to believing mothers and grandmothers.

"I remember your anguish" v. 4; "I remember your ancestry" v. 5; but more important than all this, "I remember your anointing with power by the Holy Spirit" (v. 6). Now that is a bit puzzling. What is Paul referring to? You notice that he mentions "the laying on of my hands". Turn back to 1 Timothy 4:14 – Paul says, "Do not neglect the gift you have, which was given you by prophetic utterance when the elders laid their hands on you." But now in 2 Timothy he is talking about "when I laid my hands on you". The question is whether Paul is referring to the same situation or not. In the early church they laid hands on each other much more frequently than we do today. I think we ought to do it more often. They laid hands on people on two occasions in their life. The first was right at the beginning of their Christian life and usually immediately after their baptism. They laid hands on them and prayed for the gift of the Holy Spirit's power. Usually the person who did this was the person who had led them to the Lord. Paul frequently did this and there is one example in Acts 19. He would baptise people into the name of Jesus and then, maybe soon afterwards, he would lay hands on them and pray for the gift of the Holy Spirit. Later in their Christian life, if they were called and set apart to a particular ministry of the church, whether the ministry of elder or deacon or evangelist or pastor, then on that occasion they would do the same thing again, only now the elders of the church would all lay their hands on the person and pray for a gift of the Spirit – a special gift of teaching or of ministry in some other direction. It would seem quite clear that Timothy had hands laid on him twice. The first time was right at the beginning of his Christian life when Paul laid his hands on him and prayed for the anointing of power of the Holy Spirit, which is available to all Christians. Many years later, a prophet in a church stood up and said, "Thus says the Lord, 'separate me Timothy for the ministry.'" When that was said, the elders laid their hands on Timothy and he received a gift for ministry. You see the difference? The gift of the Spirit at the beginning, a gift of ministry later on – both through the laying on of hands. Now Paul is going back to the first occasion – to that day, when Timothy came to know the Lord, was baptised and Paul himself had laid hands on him and he received power. The Greek word here is *dunamis* (the same root as "dynamite"). The same word is used of the day of Pentecost: "You shall receive power when the Holy Spirit has come upon you." Power and love – the love of God that is shed abroad by the Holy Spirit and a sound mind (or self-control). The expression "a sound mind" signifies a person whose convictions are so strong he doesn't waver, someone who knows his own mind, has a grip of himself, doesn't panic, doesn't chase around from one position to another but can stand firm even though he is alone.

Now Paul is reminding Timothy: Right at the beginning of your Christian life you didn't receive a spirit of timidity – why are you ashamed then? Why are you embarrassed to acknowledge the Lord? Why don't you testify? Why are you ashamed of the gospel? Have you forgotten that you received the spirit of power, and love, and a grip of yourself? Now that is why he is remembering this. He is recalling Timothy to that.

Then Paul begins to speak generally and he now uses the word "us" right down to v. 10, and we are included in this. For the Lord did not give us a spirit of timidity, yet how often when we get an opportunity to say a word for the Lord we sometimes miss it, feeling ashamed. The other person would probably go away and say, "Oh, he's turned religious, he's a fanatic." But God has given us a spirit of love, and when you love someone you want to talk to them about the Lord.

Paul now describes our duty, in v. 8. You can be ashamed of two things: the *message* of the gospel and the *messenger*. You can be ashamed of the message because it is centred in a cross and you can be ashamed of a messenger if he is treated like a criminal. I want you to imagine now that I have been arrested and put in jail. I want you to try to get the feel of Timothy's hesitations:

Somebody will say, "How are you getting on at your church?"

"Fairly well, thank you."

"How's your minister getting on?"

"Actually he's no longer with us."

"Where's he gone? Which church is he in now?"

"Well, he's not in a church now."

"Oh, where is he?"

"To tell you the truth he got into a bit of trouble." Now you can see how you are beginning to get thoroughly embarrassed about this.

"Oh, what sort of trouble?"

"I'm afraid he's in prison."

"You have had an odd chap for a minister. I've told you

about going to that church. You get mixed up with a lot of strange people, you know."

"But I can explain it all – the authorities misunderstood."

"Still, it doesn't sound too good, a minister in jail, does it?"

You can see how a person would be ashamed. "How is that Paul of yours?" they would say to Timothy. "Well actually, he's in prison in Rome." Ashamed of the Lord's messenger.

Timothy, don't be ashamed of the message testifying to the Lord, even if it is a cross we preach. Timothy, don't be ashamed of the Lord's messengers, even if they are treated like criminals, but take your share of suffering for the gospel. That is our duty: never to be ashamed either of the message or the messenger.

The Lord has chosen many people to use greatly of whom the world might be ashamed. As far as we know, Paul was a little man. Some people didn't like him. Yet he was the greatest missionary. John Wesley, one of the greatest Christians England has ever seen, was a little man, just over five feet, of whom nobody took any notice. It seems as if the Lord uses unknown people, cobblers like Carey and parlour-maids like Gladys Aylward – people of whom you could be ashamed very easily. Yet that's how God works, he chooses the nobodies of this world.

Paul then gives us a wonderful summary of the gospel. Let me draw out some contrasts. First: not our works, but his grace. Ages ago he promised us this, now he has let it appear in Jesus. We were dying, we were dead people, but he abolished death and brought us to life – a wonderful contrast, but the meaning is that our duty is to suffer for the gospel because the gospel saves us. After all, it was the gospel that brought you out of death into life, why not suffer for it? A gospel that saves is a gospel worth suffering for.

In v. 11 we are back again to "I and you" – very personal.

Paul is saying: for this gospel I was appointed three things: a preacher, an apostle, and a teacher. Normally there would be three different people with those gifts but Paul was a man of many gifts. A preacher is someone who goes around preaching the gospel; an apostle travelled around founding churches; a teacher is someone who comes to those churches and teaches them, builds them up in the faith. The Spirit had loaded Paul with gifts. He writes of his suffering, and you cannot be a preacher or a teacher without suffering if you are really going to give the gospel. If God appoints, you suffer. It is as simple as that. We are ordained to suffer; we are called to suffer with him. That is the badge of a true Christian – the scars of his persecution.

"But I am not ashamed." Treated like a common criminal, chained to a Roman soldier, Paul was not ashamed. I remember one day I had the privilege of walking up the Appian Way, from the Roman Port of Ostia to the city of Rome. It is a wonderful walk along the straight Roman road. It was a Sunday morning, and looking down I could see the very stones that were there two thousand years ago, and which are still there. The Romans knew how to build roads. Up that road one day there came a little Jewish man, walking between Roman guards. I wondered what he was thinking as he walked up this road. What was in his mind as he came inside that great, powerful city? The phrase I was repeating to myself all the way up that road was: "For I am not ashamed of the gospel". Little did Paul know that within three hundred years the Roman Emperor himself would be a Christian. He did not know that the Roman Empire would crumble but the church would grow, but he said "I'm not ashamed." Why is he not ashamed of the gospel? First, "I know whom I have believed." Let that sink in. Notice he doesn't say, "I know *what* I believe." A lot of people know what they believe and it doesn't help them. Paul says, "I know *whom* I have believed." If your creed is a person it is a very different thing from just believing in certain statements.

Secondly, Paul then went on to say (the end of verse twelve), "I am persuaded [or sure] that he is able to guard or keep, until that day my deposit." That is what he writes in the original Greek language, literally: "he is able to keep my deposit." People have been arguing for two thousand years as to what he meant. They split into two camps. Half say, "That means what Paul deposited with God" – namely himself. But the other half say, "It means what God deposited with Paul" – namely the gospel. So which is it that God is able to keep – the messenger or the message? – what we commit to him or what he commits to us? Both are true. You can find both truths elsewhere in scripture, but I am going to indicate which I think it really means. The Authorized Version takes this view: "He is able to keep what I've committed to him." The Revised Standard Version takes this view: "He is able to keep what he has entrusted to me" – namely the gospel.

Consider the first truth: he is able to keep what I've committed to him. That is gloriously true. When Jesus died he said, "Into your hands I deposit my spirit" – the same word translated "entrust" or "commit". The spirit of Jesus was safe in the hands of God, and so is yours. Even when you come to die, say those words if you can remember: "Into your hands I commit, deposit, entrust my spirit" and he will keep it. It is a wonderful truth, but I don't think it is the truth that Paul is wanting to express here.

I want to take the other version, namely that, "he is able to keep what he has committed to me" – the gospel. My reason for doing so is this. The word "guard" or "keep" occurs again in v. 14 where it refers to guarding not a person but the truth, the gospel. Furthermore, that same word occurs at 2:2 – "What you have heard from me before many witnesses entrust, commit, deposit to faithful men who will be able to teach others also." I think that what Paul is saying here is this: God entrusted me with the gospel, I have passed it on to you Timothy, you pass it on to someone else who will be able to teach others.

So the truth came from God to Paul, and then it is passed on. Paul means: I am quite sure that God is able to keep that gospel intact until the day that Jesus comes back. Now let that truth sink in. Think of how people have tried to alter and spoil the gospel. Catholics have added so much to it that it is like adding baggage to a canoe and it has toppled over. Protestants have taken so much away from it that there is not much of it left. Yet still, all over the world, there are groups of people who have got the gospel intact. You see, the truth is a deposit which God has deposited with us to keep and to guard intact, not to add a single thing to it, not to take away a single thing from it, but to pass it on to the people who will faithfully pass it on to others, and for two thousand years the gospel has been passed on intact. Still you can find it in the world. Paul is affirming that he is persuaded that God is able to keep that gospel going until that day when the Lord comes back – so he is not ashamed of it. It will never go out of date; it will never be old-fashioned; it will never be on the rubbish heap; it will never be discarded. Even the latest scientific textbook will be out of date in another ten years. Science is discarded but the scripture never will be. Paul was not ashamed of it because it was going to stay intact all through history. Though people alter it and spoil it and play about with the Bible, still it comes back and still people go on preaching it faithfully here and there. Truth is deposited and must be guarded. So Paul would suffer for it because it will last longer than anything else. Heaven and earth may pass away but the Word of God won't, and so we are not ashamed of it.

Now we come to the general section vv. 15–18. By the

THE PERSONAL LETTERS

way, Timothy is not only to guard the truth, he is to follow it, and that is a very different thing. It is one thing to have the Bible at your fingertips and be able to quote chapter and verse, that is just guarding the truth, but we are to follow it in faith and love. Follow it, guard it, pass it on.

Now Paul mentions a rather sad fact. He says, "You probably know that everybody in Asia has turned away from me." It must be very hard for a man who started a church to know that it has turned away from him. Phygellus and Hermogenes probably never thought they would get their names in the Bible, but they have – as deserters. But, there was one man, Onesiphorus, a devoted man, a lovely character. I would rather have one Onesiphorus in a church than a dozen like Phygellus or Hermogenes. He had served faithfully in Ephesus. When he got to Rome he searched until he found that Jewish prisoner and then he refreshed him – that is the sort of person who means a lot to you. There is an echo of the fifth beatitude here, "Blessed are the merciful for they shall obtain mercy." Onesiphorus was a merciful man, and Paul says, "May he find mercy." "I was in prison," said Jesus, "and you visited me." Onesiphorus did that for Paul.

Now thirdly, and very briefly, we look at the future. He has been endowed with the power of a sound mind (don't be ashamed); the pattern of the sound message; the pattern of sound words. Finally, he has been called up and enlisted by Christ as a soldier. A Christian must have the dedication of a soldier, the discipline of an athlete and the diligence of a farmer. Three little word pictures to be faithful: a soldier who is ready to die, to suffer for the Lord, and who doesn't get entangled with civilian pursuits but dedicates himself to the one who enlisted him; an athlete who must discipline himself and work within the rules; a farmer who must work hard and deserves the first share. All this is looking forward to the reward. This links up with an earlier verse: "I am in chains" says Paul – but you can't bind the Word of God, it goes on. I remember meeting Martin Niemöller, a German Christian who was put in solitary confinement in a concentration camp as Hitler's personal prisoner. He was allowed to keep his Bible. He had communion every Sunday morning with a little dry crust of bread and a tin mug of water, but did not see a single soul for many months. Up above his bunk there was a little grating and outside the grating, which was open to the fresh air, was the yard in which the other prisoners were exercised. They walked around this yard at five-yard intervals. As each man passed the grating he heard a whisper through it from Niemöller. To each man he gave one text, and that went on day after day after day. You can imagine the man up against the grating with his Bible. The Word of God is not bound. Hitler put Niemöller in that cell because he preached the gospel and condemned the sins that were taking place. But the Word of God is not bound and Niemöller continued preaching it. You can't shut up the Word of God even if you bind its messengers.

Finally, we come to a general promise which applies to every Christian. Do you get laughed at because you are a Christian? What do your neighbours think of you? Odd? Do they persecute you? Do you have to be embarrassed for the Lord's sake? Then if you will die with him you will live with him – you will never have God in your debt. Indeed, you may lose houses, lands, brothers and sisters, but God repays a thousand-fold. He rewards a faithful soldier, a disciplined athlete, a hardworking farmer. If we endure with him, we will reign with him. You may be humiliated by the world, you may lose your dignity because you are a Christian, but one day you will reign. Look ahead to that – you don't mind being in the dust here if you are going to reign there.

There is a promise here – but here is the other side of the promise. Jesus said: "If you're ashamed of me, I'll be ashamed of you when I come. Deny me and I'll deny you before my Father" – that is the seriousness of it. He is faithful and he keeps his word.

Read 2 Timothy 2:14–3:9

A. CORRUPTING WORDS (2:14–26)
    1. Dangerous disputes (14)
    2. Worthy workman (15)
    3. Decaying disease (16–18)
    4. Firm foundation (19)
    5. Dirty desires (20)
    6. Useful utensils (21–22)
    7. Dividing debates (23)
    8. Tender teaching (24–25)
    9. Defeated devil (25–26)

B. CORRUPTED WORKS (3:1–9)
    1. Faithlessness without precedent (2–4)
    2. Form without power (5)
    3. Followers without perception
    4. Faith without principles
    5. Folly without progress

The greatest dangers to the church come from inside and not outside it. From outside we expect attack and antagonism, but inside the church the devil would seek to worm his way in and corrupt the truth. The key word that shines out of this passage is "truth". That is what we stand for, and it is our task before Almighty God to keep the truth intact. There are two ways in which the truth can be destroyed, banished from a church: first of all through the tongue and second, through life – or through *words* and *works* that are a contradiction of the truth. I can contradict the truth by what I say or by what I do. Either way, I have attacked the truth and made it more difficult for someone else to hear it.

It may seem strange that works can contradict the truth but they can. If people outside a church can see in our lives things that contradict what we preach and teach then they will not come to know the truth, they will contradict it. Alas, both of these things can get inside a church. The latter part of chapter 2 is concerned with corrupting words that deny the truth and quibble and argue people out of the simple, plain meaning of what God has said. But in 3:1–9 we have a list of the sort of deeds that likewise corrupt the truth and destroy it. We have been looking at sound words – "sound" means "healthy", but now we are going to look at unhealthy words that can eat into the body of Christ like gangrene. That is a vivid and a horrible metaphor, but you know what Paul is getting at. Quibbling about words can be a disease in a church.

Notice certain key words here in chapter two: "words", "talk" and "chatter". In v. 23: "controversies", "quarrels". Such are things which can spoil the truth in a church: chatter, quarrels, talk not sanctified by the word of truth. The contrast is between the "words" of v. 14 and the "word" of v. 15. The truth is concerned with "the word"; falsehood is concerned with arguing – wordy battles.

The passage 2:14–26 is like one of those big sandwiches which has more than three layers. I have tried to pick out the various layers of the sandwich for you, and you will realise that Paul goes in his mind from the words of falsehood to the word of truth, from that which is wrong to that which is right. Five times he mentions this quibbling, arguing, quarrelling attitude to words, and four times he tells us what the church needs. The church needs, first of all, a worthy workman. It needs, secondly, a firm foundation. It needs, thirdly, people who are useful utensils to contain what God is wanting to fill our lives with. Fourthly, the church needs tender teachers.

A visitor once remarked about discussion groups that he had never seen any positive value in pooling our ignorance. I think all of us know the sort of discussion group that is simply argument for argument's sake – words, words, words. Paul teaches that this sort of thing does no good but it ruins the hearers. I have known people who have been turned away from the truth by argument, by discussion, by listening to Christians quibbling, and it is a very sad thing when that has happened. You may be interested that the Greek word translated "ruin" here is our English word "catastrophe" meaning to pull a thing down or "to turn it upside-down or to upset it, to demolish it. The sort of quibbling discussions that Paul has in mind "catastrophes" the hearers. It upsets them so much they never want to listen to the truth. But in contrast to those who demolish things by discussion and argument, a church needs good builders, good workmen, who will not demolish, not simply destroy the faith of hearers but strengthen it and build it up, step by step.

We now come to v. 15, a key verse. "Do your best to present yourself to God as one approved". Now one of the first things you are asked when you apply for a job is, "Have you any references? Where was your last job?" The word "approved" means here "references". A workman can say, "Here's my reference. Here's my last boss's opinion of me." Study; do your best. It means: be zealous to present yourself to God a workman with references, approved, qualified, skilled, apprenticed.

Now we come to the two things a workman needs: pride in his work, and proficiency in it. Isn't it lovely to meet someone who takes a pride in his work? I can tell you how you can spot it. When he has finished a job, he will stand back and look at it. If he has done a bad job, he will get as far away from it as he can, as quickly as he can. But a man who has done a good job will stand back. If there is something wrong with it, he will return to it and work at it until it is right. The good workman so handles his tools that he can stand back and say, "I've done a good job." He can let anyone come and look at it, and he will not be ashamed or embarrassed. He won't say, "Well, I'm afraid that was a poor bit of timber just there." He'll be proud, stand there and let anyone inspect his work. Our Bible study is to be like that. We are so to study the scriptures that we are not ashamed of what we say about them. We don't rush through it, we are proud of our workmanship because we have done it properly. We have studied hard; we have done our best. Now you cannot take a pride in your workmanship unless you have proficiency in it, and that never comes quickly. Some people, I am afraid, want to be able to do a thing straight away. You hear a great pianist, and think, "Oh, if only I could do that," and you have three lessons, and it is so discouraging at first. There is only one way to get proficiency and that is to do a thing again and again and again. It is the only way you will be proficient in handling scripture. The Bible is a complicated book. It has so many truths in it you will spend all your lifetime with it and still say, "I don't understand it all." But little and often, as you study it again and again, you begin to handle your tools properly. You begin to be able to use the Word of God to do a skilful job in helping other people.

At 2:15, the Authorized Version (AV/KJV) reads: "rightly dividing the word of truth" but this is more accurately rendered: "rightly handling". I am not quibbling but there has been misunderstanding here. The AV has an unfortunate translation of the word, for Paul never intended this to mean "cutting up the word into bits" or dividing one part of the word from another part. The word he uses actually means "straight-cutting'. Whenever you get a double word like that it is the first part of it which is the important word. For example, if I say, "You can get to central London on the underground" I have used a double word, "underground," and I am not talking about the ground but about *under*. You see, the first part of the word is the important part, and in "straight-cutting," the emphasis is not in the cutting but on the straight. Indeed, there are eight other words in the Greek language for dividing a thing into pieces, which Paul could have used had that been his meaning, and this word does not mean dividing. Straight-cutting means "to plough a straight furrow."

Now I remember the first day I ploughed, and I am ashamed of it! When I got to the end of the row and looked back, it was appalling. You would think I had been drunk! The word is used of a man who cuts a straight road through the hills or a straight path through his garden. It is used of a man who cuts a stone for a building and cuts it absolutely straight. In other words, the emphasis here is not in dividing at all but on skilled straight-cutting. If you get a block of wood and a saw, and without drawing a line on it, cut it through, see how straight it is. You are a straight-cutter if you can skilfully handle your tools. Therefore, the right translation is "rightly handling the word of truth". Paul uses this phrase, "the word of truth" twice elsewhere, and he is not referring to the scriptures, he is referring to the gospel. In Ephesians and Colossians he says, "The word of truth which is the gospel". The workman God wants is one who can handle skilfully, accurately, and preach in a straightforward, straight and accurate manner the word of truth, which is the gospel. You don't get that easily; you get it by studying and studying the word of truth.

Now I am afraid we return to this disease of godless chatter. Any discussion that is not centred on the word of God is a waste of time, but people love discussion groups. They love red herrings and they love to bring up their own ideas and grind their own axes. The word "chatter" here is the word "babbling" or "babel-ing". You get the same sort of confusion from godless chatter as you got at the Tower of Babel, the tower of chatter, confusion, when nobody understood anybody else – it is the same word.

Unfortunately there were two people who were doing this in the church where Timothy was, and their names have got into the Word of God as those who could not keep straight: "They have swerved from the truth." If you cannot handle a saw, I guarantee that if you were sawing a long plank down the middle and didn't draw a line, you would swerve. It is one of the things that an amateur joiner will inevitably do. The amateur won't get his shoulder in line with his hand, and he starts down the plank and begins to swerve away. This is what these two people were doing. They were not straight-cutting, they were not skilful, they swerved from the truth, and they were teaching all sorts of weird theories. For example, you know that Christ is coming back to earth. You look forward to it and so do I. But if you get a Jehovah's Witness on your doorstep, he will tell you that you have missed it – that Christ came in 1918. Now you can work this out for yourself, but the person teaching on your doorstep is saying that the thing to which we are looking forward has already happened! That is swerving from the truth, not straight-cutting, not skilful handling of the Word of God. Hymenaeus and Philetus had taken another event to which Christians look forward – the resurrection of the body, which has not happened yet, but they said, "It's happened already, and you've missed it." They could prove it from the way they handled the Word. Do you know, if you don't handle the Word carefully and skilfully, you can prove almost anything you like from it? If you have made up your mind about a thing first and then start reading the Bible, you can make the Bible prove what you thought before you read it. This is where swerving and unskilful handling has done so much damage. I don't fear those who give us their own opinions and deny Christian faith by their ideas, but I am terribly afraid of those who give us their ideas and make the Bible prove them – they are the dangerous people.

Some get awfully confused with this and say, "How can you tell? You see, here's this person on my doorstep. They've got a Bible in their hands and they quote this, that and the other. Here is somebody else, and they quote the Bible, and these people contradict one another. How do I know? My faith is being upset. I just can't understand all this." Of course, this is what Hymenaeus and Philetus were doing – they were upsetting the faith, taking away the foundation on which people's faith is built.

What are we to do when this happens? The answer is that there is a firm foundation, something you can build on, something you can be sure of. In fact there are two things. Many church buildings have foundation stones with inscriptions on them. The idea of Paul is that the church's foundation has a sure inscription on it. Two things you can be sure of: first, that *God can sort out the true from the false*.

He knows those who are his. You hear all these different interpretations, but don't get worried because God knows which is the right one and one day he is going to sort it out. The other thing is this: we know which is the right one too, because *everyone who is truly teaching the truth will depart from iniquity*.

Our Lord warned in the Sermon on the Mount that false preachers would come dressed not as wolves but as sheep. Sheep are the people of God. So our Lord warned his followers that people would come into the church – professing Christians – who would be false prophets. How do you identify them? By their fruits. If that man is not growing in grace and himself getting nearer to God and living a holier life, then you know he is not truly a teacher because a true teacher cannot but teach himself while he teaches others. If a person really teaches the Word of God, he feels uncomfortable for himself every time – it hits the preacher as much as the congregation. A true teacher will take note of what he teaches himself and do something about it.

So you need not worry that there are false teachers. God knows those who are his, and we have a test. What is his life like? Is he leading people to more godliness or less? Looking back to v. 16, a false teacher will lead people further from God and into ungodliness, and his life will be less holy than before. But a teacher who is from God will raise the standard of living and holiness so that we need not be upset. This is the firm foundation.

Interestingly, there is an echo in this verse of an incident in Numbers 16 in which a man called Korah, together with Dathan, Abiram and On rose up against Moses. Their complaint was: Moses, you have gone too far. You are running this people; you are lording it over us, and we don't like it. We feel that we ought to be having a say in things. They were, of course, simply rebelling against God's

THE PERSONAL LETTERS

leadership. Moses said to them: "God will show who is his." On the next day, Moses said, "Now keep away from these people. Those who are camping around these men, lift your tents up and move them further away because God is going to do something about them." The dreadful story ends with an earthquake in which that particular part of that camp opened up. Those men were swallowed up in the cracks of the earth. God showed those who were his. The only reason I noticed that they were told to move their tents away from those people was lest they be dragged down with them when the earthquake occurred. Undoubtedly, Paul is thinking of that incident. God will show ultimately; God will judge. You had better keep away from people who rebel because sooner or later God will deal with them, and if you are too close to them you might find he is dealing with you too.

So we are given our firm foundation but now we move on to the matter of dirt – dirty dirt, not clean dirt. Clean dirt is the dirt you can wash off. Nobody is worried about clean dirt. Our Lord wasn't worried. It was said to him, "Your disciples haven't washed their hands before eating." Jesus made it clear that it is far more important that we should be clean inside than clean outside, though most of us spend all the time on the outside. So let us look at clean dirt and dirty dirt here. In a large house there are vessels, utensils of all shapes and sizes: jars, buckets, bins. Some of them are clean and can be used for anything at all. A vessel that is clean can hold anything. But there are some vessels in your house that cannot be used for anything because they are dirty vessels – like your rubbish bin. The interesting thing is that you can use a dirty vessel for only a very limited number of purposes, but you can use a clean vessel for anything at all. Here is another interesting thing: in your house (at least I hope this is true) the dirty vessels and the clean ones you keep separately. If you keep them all on the same shelf you are asking for trouble. Paul is telling Timothy that in the church Christ needs people who are clean vessels so that he can put anything he wants in that person and use them for any purpose he desires. If they are dirty vessels, he may be able to use them but only for certain limited purposes, whereas he wants vessels that are ready for any good work.

The sort of dirt that he has in mind here is quite obvious from v. 22 – "Shun youthful passions". Those are not only the passions of lust and other things; they are the passions of ambition and novelty. Young people love anything new, but after a few weeks they are worn out. The passion of impatience; the passion of argument. Shun youthful passions – they make a vessel dirty, and God cannot use it for anything. Therefore, a useful utensil to God must be two things: it must be *clean* and it must be *consecrated*, ready for anything. If you want God to use you for himself, then make sure that you are clean and consecrated.

Here again there is a point of variation. The beginning of v. 21 tells us how to get clean: "If anyone purifies himself from what is ignoble...." The big question, and I must try to be absolutely straight-cutting here, is whether this means that we are to be separate from dirt or from dirty dishes. In other words, whether it is dirty things that Paul has in mind or dirty people. I am still thinking of moral dirt, not clean dirt. After studying this very carefully, I think Paul means both. It is obvious that a Christian's first job is to keep himself clean. Before ever he starts pulling specks out of other people's eyes, he has to deal with the beam in his own. A Christian's first task is to make sure that he is clean from these things that spoil a man or woman for God's use. But on the other hand, the exact words of this v. 21 carry the clear implication that if there is a fellow Christian, a vessel, who is obviously dirty, then for the sake of the Lord, you should keep away from him.

The first word that tells us this is *purify*, which is only used one other time in the New Testament, in 1 Corinthians 5, where a man in a church was guilty of a very dirty thing. The rest of the church was told to purify itself of that man for there is nothing that can damage the truth more than an obviously dirty person in the church who is known by all and yet not dealt with by the church.

I knew a church which was noted for its Christian testimony until one member was publicly dirty in this sense. Because the church did not do what it should have done and discipline that member straightaway – in love, with firm discipline – but allowed that to continue, the church lost its reputation for holiness in the district. It means both that a Christian has first a solemn responsibility to be clean himself and that a church has a responsibility to deal with dirty vessels that are sitting alongside the clean. I cannot get round that meaning here.

The other word that settles it, I think, is that in fact Paul says, "If anyone purifies himself from these..." – in other words, the vessels that have given themselves to ignoble, dirty use. But now we notice that while we are to be clean and seek to be filled with righteousness, faith, love and peace, we are to seek this with the clean vessels. In other words, a Christian has a duty not to be too closely attached to dirty vessels, but he also has a duty to be very closely attached to the clean vessels and to seek to be filled along with the clean.

All this is not talking about unbelievers; it is not talking about people who aren't Christians. It is talking about vessels in the house, and we are never told, for example, not to eat with an unbeliever. But we are told not to eat with a believer who is deliberately, by his own choice, a dirty vessel – that is a very different thing. Paul says to the Corinthians that we have no right or responsibility whatever to judge those who are outside the church, but it is our task to judge those who are inside. You do not cut yourself off because someone is not a brother but because he is a dirty vessel by his own choice, and you are hoping by this to bring him back to be a clean vessel.

Verse 23 returns to those debates again – loving arguments; v. 24 goes back to the thing the church needs. What do we do about these people who teach these silly things? Here is the hardest thing of all. On the one hand, you can win your argument with them and lose them. On the other hand, you can lose your argument and win them. But the most difficult thing to do, and the thing that we are supposed to do, is to win the argument and win the person. When you meet a false teacher – a man, for example, who is teaching that Christ was not born of a virgin or that the miracles did not happen – you have three choices. You can argue with him until you win, and he goes off in a huff and resentful, and you have lost your man. You can give into him and say, "Well, I think you're right," and you might gain your man, but you lose your argument, and the truth is gone. But the most difficult thing of all is so to speak to him that you both win your argument and win the person. How do you do that? By correcting him, speaking to him of what is right. You have got to do that – it is a duty, but it will largely be concerned with the manner in which you do it. If you do it in a fighting spirit, with a quarrelsome attitude, in a harsh or overbearing manner, then you will win your argument and lose the person. If, on the other hand, your manner is so gentle that you never correct him, you will win him and lose your argument. But if you correct him with gentleness and kindliness but tell him quite clearly where he is wrong, then you may both win your argument and the person. Then you have got him out of the snare of the devil. The devil has lost someone that he got a grip of – because the devil is after even our Lord's disciples. After all, out of twelve disciples, he got hold of Judas and he nearly got hold of Simon Peter. The devil's trick is to get hold of Christians and swerve them from the truth – and a kindly teacher might bring them back and teach them what is right.

There has been a little debate about who "him" and "his" refer to at the end of 2:26. Some have said both refer to the devil and mean: after being captured by the devil, to do the devil's will. Others think it means: after being captured by the teacher to do God's will – and still others think it means: after being captured by God, to do God's will. All three are true. There is nothing much at stake in the divided opinion there.

Now we come to something different yet related. Sooner or later, corrupted words lead to corrupted works. Sooner or later false teaching leads to false living, and here we have the other side. We will look at five things in chapter three. Firstly, look at v. 1. The two phrases that are important are "the last days" (and we must ask when that refers to) and secondly the word "times". Some have thought that "last days" referred to the very end of human history, but that is not so. While there is a partial truth in that, it would be quite silly for Paul to tell Timothy: in the last days certain things will happen; now you see that you avoid such things – because Timothy did not live in the final days of history. But as for the last period of history which began with Christ, we are already in that. Do you remember on the day of Pentecost how Peter announced that in the *last days* God would pour out his Spirit? We have been living in the last days for two thousand years and we are still in them. While it is true that the features of the last days will get worse and worse until they reach a climax at the end, the things mentioned here we have been experiencing for two thousand years and are going to experience. In this period of history, the last two thousand years, "the last days", Paul says that there will be times of real strain for Christians. I solemnly believe that in this country of England we are entering such a time of stress. What happens in such a time? First of all, men will be *fierce* – that is the word used in the middle of this horrible list. Without precedent, things that never happened before in human history will happen. Look at this list – it is a ghastly list of what godlessness is. I want you to notice the first thing in it and the last: lovers of self rather than lovers of God. Do you know what sin is? Sin is wrongly directed love – that is all. For when God made us, he made us capable of loving, and you either love him or you love self. A person who loves self is a sinner, and whether they are a crude or a refined sinner does not matter. A person who loves God is a righteous man or woman.

The times of stress come when people do not love God any more, they just love themselves. Are we not in such a time of stress? You see, if you love self, then secondly you become a lover of money. You can't help that because if you are looking after number one, the first thing you need in this world is money. If you are a lover of self rather than a lover of God, then I will guarantee that you will begin to want more and more money. So it becomes a drug. When you get more money, then you become proud and arrogant. "I've got a bigger bank balance; I've got a bigger house." You begin to feel better than others. You can see how it goes. This list is progressive, getting worse and worse: you become abusive, insulting other people.

"Disobedient to parents" – that indicates a time of stress, and I think it is more difficult to bring up children and teenagers today than it was. We are in such a time of stress when our own young people are surrounded by others who care nothing for parental discipline or respect. Somebody asked me, "Which is the most difficult period of childhood?" I don't know; I think every one of them. But perhaps fourteen to eighteen is one of the most difficult. "Ungrateful" – well

THE PERSONAL LETTERS

that goes with disobedience to parents. You no longer feel grateful to them for all they have done for you. You just want to get away from them, treat your home as a boarding house.

"Unholy" – all of these are the opposite of virtues. "Inhuman, implacable" – which means someone who falls out and will not be reconciled. "Slanderous, gossips, profligate, fierce, haters of good" – when you have got to this point you cannot stand a good person. You feel so uncomfortable and you just don't like them. You hate anything good and you hate a person who is good. "Treacherous, reckless, swollen with conceit" and then, as if to cap it all, "lovers of pleasure rather than lovers of God". I can prove to you in just one sentence that we are in such a time of stress. How do people behave on Sunday – as lovers of pleasure or lovers of God? That is the simple proof we are in a time of stress.

The next surprising thing this chapter tells us is that such people still like religion and will have fashionable, crowded churches. This is astonishing. Man is a religious creature, and even though he is living for money, even though he is living for pleasure, living for himself, wrapped up in himself, some still like to go to church. You will get, with this fashionable churchgoing, reciting of the creeds, all the form and appearance of religion, but without the dynamite. You see, what is the gospel? It is the power of God unto salvation. You go to a fashionable church where people are these things and preach the gospel of salvation to them, and they will deny it. They will say, "That's nothing to do with Christianity; we don't want "hot gospelling" in here. We don't want that sort of thing." Speak to them of the Holy Spirit and they either don't know what you are talking about or they say, "No, I don't think such things are for today." Denying the *power* – it is the same word, "You shall receive *power* when the Holy Spirit is come upon you." The only Christianity that is worth calling Christianity is Holy Spirit Christianity that has power in it and not just the form of religion.

Alas, these people who are corrupted in their works will be inside church, but you will not see the power of the Holy Spirit in them. If you talk to them of the Holy Spirit's power to sanctify, they will deny it. It is not what they want in their religion. They want the form or the fashion of religion. "Avoid such people," says Paul to Timothy. "Don't get mixed up with people like that." Fashionable religion can go along with love of self, love of money, love of pleasure, but that is not Christianity – it is the form without the power.

Such people invariably (vv. 6–7) can make their way into households and capture weak women. Ever since the Garden of Eden it has been easier to deceive some women in relation to the truth than others. This is invariably where false teaching gets a hold. Do you notice that a sect calling at doors will get hold of the wife, talk her into it, tie her up in their teaching, and poor soul, she has fallen for it. Now this is wrong, and this is why it is always wise to witness to husband and wife together wherever you get the opportunity. Such people worm their way into households and get hold of these women who are wanting the sensational rather than the serious, who listen to anybody, and who never arrive at the truth. That is the pity of it, and you know, the next person who comes along with some different teaching, they will follow. This is the sort of way that such false teaching spreads.

Two magicians, Jannes and Jambres, opposed the truth. Do you remember when Moses went to Pharaoh's court? Moses did a miracle, and the magicians of Pharaoh did miracles too. Counterfeit faith – it is so easy for a person to counterfeit the things of God by the devil's power. There is nothing real that cannot be counterfeited. There is not a gift of the Spirit that cannot be counterfeited. There is not a thing that God does that cannot be counterfeited, and when it is counterfeited by men of corrupt mind you have got the same situation as Moses had: faith without principles – they have faith; they believe they can do anything. They have tremendous self-confidence.

But now in v. 9 there is comfort for you amidst all this. Even though there will be such false leaders leading women astray, the final truth is that they won't get very far. For a time they will be successful and grow and spread, but sooner or later people see through it. The only thing that will survive is truth. You can read through the last two thousand years of church history, the last days, and you will find that every false teaching has finally crumbled, people have turned away from it and the truth has gone on. It is very comforting to know that folly will not ultimately triumph. That gives me tremendous comfort in this way: that if I am giving the truth, then it won't fade away, and that if people come to the truth, their progress will go on regardless of their teachers, once they have the Holy Spirit within them. He is the Teacher. This is the difference, then, that false teaching only goes for a time and then it collapses. You will find churches that have collapsed and disappeared because false teaching got in, but now they have gone and it is over and done with. So false teaching is awfully dangerous, but it is not permanent, and it goes, and the truth goes marching on.

That brings us through this rather difficult section of 2 Timothy. Just let me pull the threads together. I have tried to show you that the truth is the important thing and that there are two things that can eat away at the truth and take it out of a church. One is wordiness, false teaching – words, words, words. After you have listened to these people, you say, "What on earth are they saying? What are they trying to teach? It's just words, words." On the other hand, there are those whose works and whose lives – even though they have the form of godliness, even though they are in church on Sunday – are patently away from God. These are two things to watch, but the comfort is that neither of them can ultimately get too far. All of them are under God's restraining hand. There comes a point where God says, "That's enough of that" – and it comes to an end, and the truth goes on.

Read 2 Timothy 3:10 – 4:22

A. THE LORD RESCUES (10–13)
   1. My suffering (10–11)
   2. Inevitable for godliness (12–13)

B. THE LORD EQUIPS (14–17)
   1. Your scripture (14–15)
   2. Inspired by God (16–17)

C. THE LORD JUDGES (1–5)
   1. Your preaching (1–2)
   2. Criticised by men (3–5)

D. THE LORD REWARDS (6–8)
   1. My prize (6–8a)
   2. Crowned for merit (8b)

Paul's final words
               i. His personal companions
               ii. His practical needs
               iii. His pending trial

There are four things to which I want to draw your attention now – fundamental things in the Christian life. First, the Lord rescues us from all evil – that is a wonderful truth for the Christian. You will suffer for your Christian life, but the Lord will rescue you from all your suffering. Second, you are going to be in a battle, not a picnic and, like every soldier you need equipment. Paul is reminding young Timothy that the Lord equips you. Some people say, "What's the point of having a Bible school? I can't think why they spend so much time on the Bible at your church. Why do they do it? This is beginning to get out of proportion, surely?" The answer is that every Sunday morning we report to the Quartermaster's stores for our equipment and the Lord equips us for the week by our Bible study. If that doesn't happen then there is either something wrong in our frame of mind as we come – if we are just coming as a duty or for entertainment – or there is something wrong with the teaching. The third truth is that the Lord judges everything you and I do for him. One day we are to be tested: me in my teaching, all of us in our Christian service. The fourth truth is that the Lord awards prizes – crowns for those who have been faithful in this matter. If you can remember those four things, you have got four wonderful truths for the Christian life.

Now let us go through them. Under each of these truths, there are two thoughts, one particular and personal to either Paul or Timothy, and the other quite general, applying to all Christians. For example under the first, Paul talks about "*my* suffering" – that is personal. Then he makes a general statement that "*all* who live a godly life" will suffer persecution. Then he talks about Timothy: your knowledge of the scripture which you have had from a child. That is a

THE PERSONAL LETTERS

particular truth about Timothy. Then he gives a general truth: all scripture is inspired of God and can equip anyone for the same task. Then he talks about Timothy's preaching – that is personal. After that, a general truth: that the time is coming when preaching will be unpopular. We are certainly in that time. Fourth, he goes back again to himself and talks about his own prize that is waiting for him – Paul, in the future. Then he makes a general statement: the prize is waiting for all who love Christ's appearing.

The next thing to notice about the whole passage is that links are made. [Paul's] *suffering* is linked up with his *prize* – the crown he is going to get is because he has suffered and kept faithful. The Bible is connected with preaching: that is what you are to preach – the inspired Word of God. There is a wonderful pattern emerging in this (as far as we know) last letter of Paul. These are the four most important thoughts that he wanted to leave in our minds: our *suffering*, from which the Lord will rescue us; our *task*, for which the Lord will equip us; our *preaching and teaching*, for which the Lord will judge us; and our *faithfulness*, for which the Lord will reward us.

Let us look at Paul's suffering. He writes, "Now you have observed my teaching." The word "observed" is rather interesting. I remember when I first went to work on the farm. The first really skilled task I was taught was how to stack corn. You might think it looks easy enough – you just pile up sheaves on top of each other and make a nice shape. It looks simple until you try it. Believe me, the first time you try it you get about three layers on and then it seems to start sliding. You keep one foot on one bit while you put another on top and then the whole thing collapses. I was put with a man who was well into his sixties who was the master stacker on the farm. He said, "Now you just follow me around and watch what I do. Watch how I turn them in, watch how I bind them in." He made me watch carefully what he did so that I could learn to do it. After a bit, I began to learn how to do the job. The word "observed" here is exactly the word used for an apprentice who has been told to watch the expert in order to see how to do it. Paul is saying to Timothy: you have observed certain things in me, you have been my apprentice – you have watched how I did things so that you could be an expert too; you have watched my teaching. The quickest way to learn to be a good Christian teacher is indeed to watch somebody else teaching. He also says, "You've watched my conduct." For it is no use if a man's conduct does not back up his teaching. I think that I learned more about the ministry by observing an experienced minister than during three years of college. I watched his conduct. You don't know what someone's aim in life is until you watch that person closely. He might be at church on Sunday, but that doesn't mean that his aim in life is to please God. It might mean that his aim in life is to get on in business or to be popular. Paul sets out his aim in life clearly. Timothy had watched Paul's faith, patience, love, steadfastness, and above all his persecutions and sufferings. If you are going to be an expert Christian, you must watch this point of suffering.

Now Paul mentions three places in which he suffered: Antioch, Iconium, and Lystra. Why only those three? He had been shipwrecked here, stoned there, flogged there, put into prison there, hungry somewhere else. Yet here he only mentions these three places – why? The answer is that these are the three towns in Timothy's home district. He is saying: "Timothy you remember the day they dragged me out of Lystra and they threw stones at me until they thought they had killed me. Then they left me lying – bleeding, bruised, and broken in the road outside Lystra. You remember that, Timothy, don't you?" Now comes the truth: every single Christian who would live a godly life in Christ Jesus is going to suffer. This does not mean that every Christian suffers, because I am afraid there are Christians who don't want to live godly lives and don't want holiness. But the word is that not some but *all* who would live a *godly* life in Christ Jesus will suffer.

Why should that be? The answer is firstly that you will be different. Your neighbours don't live godly lives, they live ungodly lives. You might be the sort of Christian who would keep your Christianity to the church and your home and never let on to the neighbours that you are different. But if you really want to live a godly life, you are going to be so different they won't like you so much. You won't fit in easily. Someone who had only just come to know the Lord told me that straightaway they found they couldn't join in the sort of jokes that were told in the office. They were different. When you come to that point, you either snigger and join in the jokes and deny your Lord or you live a godly life in Christ Jesus and you say, "I'm afraid I don't think that's funny." If you do that, you are going to suffer. Don't be surprised when this sort of thing occurs. Indeed, "Blessed are you when men shall say all manner of evil falsely against you for my sake. Rejoice and be exceedingly glad for so persecuted they the prophets which were before you," said Jesus.

Paul, like Jesus, was absolutely honest. He did not promise people an easy passage. Wherever he went he preached that through much tribulation, or trouble, we must enter the kingdom of God. Paul teaches Timothy: you have seen my suffering and if you follow me as an apprentice, you will suffer too. These days, people may not stone us to death, but they laugh and criticise, they tease and avoid; they talk about us behind our backs. But in many parts of the world, the suffering of Christians does involve martyrdom, even today.

The other reason why we are bound to suffer is that evil people are going to go from bad to worse (see v. 13). The world is not going to get better; it is going to get worse. Godless people are going to become more and more ungodly. That is the future of our culture, and therefore the more we go on in history, the more different we shall be from them. People don't like others who are different.

Now let us turn to that lovely truth: from all these the Lord *rescued* me. Does that mean Paul never suffered? No, but it does mean that he came through the suffering to continue his ministry. The word "rescue" is not to bring you *out* of something, but to bring you *through* it. There is a certain kind of religion that wants to be rescued out of everything – rescued out of ill health, rescued out of worries, rescued out of troubles, rescued out of burdens. But the Bible teaches that the Lord's rescue is bringing you through them. He did not rescue Paul out from the stoning at Lystra – they left him, thinking he was dead from his wounds. God rescued him through it. Paul went on preaching. He is later going to write, "The Lord will rescue me from every evil" (see 4:18).

Facing certain death, how can he say, "The Lord will rescue me from every evil"? When I walk through the valley of the shadow of death, it is not from death I need to be preserved, but from evil. I will fear no *evil*. Even when it comes time to die, no evil can touch the one the Lord rescues. Isn't that a lovely truth? He will rescue you from every evil. Even though you suffer, even though you die as a martyr, the Lord rescues you from every evil.

Next we turn to our equipping. If you are going to stand up to suffering and be ready to face persecution you need equipment because you will have to fight. The equipment that you need is the scriptures. For a preacher, here is a sermon with five points: what, who, when, why and how. What is your equipment? It is what you have learned and firmly believe. Notice that it is not just enough to learn the Bible – it is *firmly believed*. Some people can learn and quote verses. I remember as a child going in for a scripture exam. I learned Paul's missionary journeys inside out. I learned it and I think I got a prize, but I still did not *firmly believe* it. But when you learn the Bible *and* firmly believe it, you are equipped.

We remember Timothy had learnt from his mother and grandmother – two godly women who did the finest thing they could do for him. Today I go into homes where parents are very anxious about their child's education in the right school, have the right friends and good opportunities. Yet the one thing those parents don't do for the child is equip them for life. Well, when do you start? I hear parents say, "I'm not going to give my child religion until they're old enough to decide." So I say to them, "I presume you don't give them any food either, do you?" They are horrified! It is utterly ridiculous to say, "I'll wait until they're old enough before I give them any religion." They wouldn't do that for their physical condition and they wouldn't do it for their mental condition, so why do it for their spiritual condition? The word is, literally: from *infancy*, Timothy, you have had this equipment. What a privilege to have had that. Mind you, it does not mean that a person who has been through a Bible school is a Christian; it just means they have got the equipment. Why? Well, because the Bible can do something for you which no other book can do. It can tell you everything you need to know for salvation, and its only purpose is to lead you to faith in Christ Jesus. In other words, you come to a person through the book. When you trust him, the Bible is the best book you can read to make you wise. An Evangelical differs from many other Christians in that he believes that the whole Bible is God's book – that it is not just a human book but is to be absolutely trusted from cover to cover, a book with final authority over everything I believe and everything I do, because it has been inspired by God.

2 Timothy 3:16 is an important verse. Alas, the translation of it has been a subject of argument. In two versions it begins, "All scripture is inspired by God and profitable". But a footnote in the RSV indicates that another translation is possible: "Every scripture inspired by God is also profitable." That was the translation of the RV of 1880 and the NEB of 1961. At first sight there is nothing to choose between these two translations – it could be either. But, unfortunately, that second one has been taken by some to mean that there are scriptures which are not inspired and that only the inspired parts are profitable. This might sound like quibbling over words to you, but a lot hangs on it. Either this whole book is inspired by God and profitable or only the inspired parts of it are profitable. Which does Paul mean? Fortunately, there can be no doubt about what he means. Until the beginning of the nineteenth century no-one, Jew or Christian, questioned that this book was inspired from cover to cover. But, later on, some people began to feel that there were parts of it that were purely human and that many parts of it were not profitable to read. I remember a minister of the church saying to me, "I never preach Leviticus; I've never been able to find anything in it." He felt it was an uninspired and unprofitable part of scripture. So when it came to 1880, the Revised Version translators preferred the other translation because it didn't commit you to a view that the whole scripture was inspired, but only that inspired bits are profitable. The NEB did the same for the same reason. In Paul's mind there would have been no question that every Old Testament passage is inspired of God, and, through most of Christian history, Christians, whether Catholic or Protestant, believed in the inspiration of the *whole* Bible. Paul makes the statement he does for this reason: only someone who really believes that the Bible is the inspired Word of God will find it profitable for his equipment.

Let us look at this word "inspired". It means "God breathed" – literally "God spirited" or "God winded". Now somebody says, "Oh, but surely this is a human book, human authors; you can see their styles. You can see what Paul thought about a thing, what John thought." Well, look at it this way. One day God took of the dust of the earth and he made a body with it. Then he breathed into it and it became something quite different – a living soul. Now according to a chemist, I am worth maybe a couple of pounds on the open market! In other words, if you could reduce my body to sugar, fat, minerals and then sell it, that is all I am worth. That is the dust of the earth, that is looking at me clearly as an earthly being, but I am worth far more than that because *God* breathed. That makes me quite different from a little bit of the dust of the earth. It is true that human authors took a pen and wrote. It is true that over forty of them wrote little bits and not one of them knew he was writing the Bible. But it is also true that God breathed into it all and that makes it something quite different. So those who treat this as a purely human book and feed it into a computer have missed the real truth. They come out with their computer answers and they say, "There, that's the truth about the Bible" – and they have missed it. Just as a scientist who says I am worth a couple of pounds' worth of chemicals has missed the truth because those chemicals will one day go back to the earth and be finished with, but I go up. Lazarus died and he was carried by the angels to Abraham's bosom. His body wasn't – the chemicals were finished with. One day, books made of paper and printer's ink will be finished with. When we get to heaven, there won't be Bibles but the Word of God will still be there, for that is what was breathed by God.

That is why I think so highly of the Bible – why, as some have said, I've got "Bible mania". That is why I will not preach anything but those things that I can find in scripture.

Because I can tell you something that nobody else in the world can tell you – not how to be educated, not how to be clever, but how to be *wise unto salvation*. Then you are equipped and you can go out and fight your battles. You can face this coming week. You can face the suffering. You can live a godly life because you have been equipped. Put it like this: if I ask you, "Tell me who you think is a man of God or a woman of God and let's go and ask that person, 'What do you do with your Bible?'" you will find that a man of God is a man of the book. It always goes together. You cannot be equipped without the Bible. It is "useful for teaching, for reproof, for correction, and training."

Now we come to the future: Timothy's preaching. Paul starts with a solemn charge: "I charge you, in the presence of God and of Christ Jesus who is to judge the living and the dead, and by his appearing and his kingdom, preach the word."

The most subtle temptation that every preacher faces is to think of what the congregation would like him to preach. That is a real battle. Believe me, you can see almost everything from the pulpit. It is really difficult to say something when I can see some sitting in a congregation on drawing pins and hating it. A little voice says, "Rush over this point." It is so very easy to say, "Well now, this will upset somebody." They came to our Lord and they said, "Did you know that they were offended at that saying?" From time to time somebody says, "Well somebody was offended at that; they don't like coming to this church." Jesus said, "Whatever my Father has not planted will be rooted up." In other words, the offence is because a person is not thoroughly planted by God. The preacher's temptation is to think that he stands before the bar of the congregation's judgment in his preaching.

Timothy is reminded that in his preaching he is responsible

to God alone for what he says, not to any man. Better be thrown out of a church for preaching what God wants to preach than to be rejected in "that Day" because one has not preached what the Lord wanted. "Timothy, I charge you before the Christ who judges, preach the word" and I favour the AV word here, the *instant* – in season and out of season. That word "instant" has come back into common use. It means something that is ready for immediate use at any occasion. Not something that is being used all the time, but ready in a moment. Preach the word and you will be instant. So if you meet somebody in need and the opportunity occurs to say a word for Jesus, you don't need to go back and check up in your books and then go back to the person. You are instant – you are preaching the word. You tell them about Jesus.

Sometimes you can preach the word out of season when you thought, "This is a situation I just cannot witness in" and suddenly you find you can, and an instant preacher jumps in. We are to do it to convince, to rebuke and to exhort. Of those three only the third is popular. To rebuke is not very popular. Said someone to a fellow worker in a factory who was swearing using the name of Christ, "Do you mind not using that name like that? You're speaking about someone I love." That is being an instant preacher; that is rebuking. It is not easy or popular.

Be unfailing in patience. Never get irritated because they won't listen, annoyed because they are so slow to learn, weary because you preach so much and so little goes in, despairing because in a church meeting someone says something that would almost seem to imply that they have not taken in a single sermon for years. Paul tells Timothy never to be impatient. Some people are fools and slow to believe all that the prophets have said. For the time is coming when congregations will choose preachers to their own liking. What set of preachers do you think they will choose? The first characteristic is that they will be brief. People who will sit for hours watching a television and for two hours watching a film or a concert, yet find twenty minutes too long for the Word of God. So a congregation with itching ears accumulates for themselves brief teachers to suit their own likings – novel teachers who are not saying something true, but something new – a new fancy every week. They like flattering teachers who will not tell you how bad you are but how good you are; comforting teachers, who will never challenge; learned teachers who have an academic atmosphere about them – "emptying the church by degrees" that has been called. Above all, they want teachers who are more interested in fiction than in fact, so that a congregation wanders away from the truth into myths.

That is going to happen and it is very difficult. There are several temptations in a day when so many congregations choose preachers of their own liking rather than those who stand before God and say, "I know that I'm going to answer to you for what I say to them this morning, not to them." They may criticise. They may go away and say, "I don't like it, it is not very nice."

Verse 5 sums up what is needed: be steady, endure suffering, do the work of the evangelist, fulfil your ministry.

Verses 6–8 are very personal. Paul knows he is going to die by execution. "I'm about to be sacrificed." I wonder if you have ever seen a sacrifice. It is not very pleasant to see an animal having its throat slit. Paul had stood on the very spot outside the gate of the Roman city wall where he would kneel and bow his head forward for the Roman executioner to slice it off with a sword. He says, "The point of my departure is at hand," and the word "departure" is interesting. It is, literally, "the point of my loosing". The word Paul uses is for pulling up your tent pegs, or a ship pulling up its anchor before it launches out into the deep. Paul knew the time had come for him to pull up his tent pegs, pull up the anchor and go out into the great deep. The time had come for him to die.

Now he says three things, all in the perfect tense. If you really learn and firmly believe the Word of God, when you get to the end of the road, and if you are given the privilege of dying in your own bed, with your relatives around, you will be able to say three things to them: "I have fought the good fight, I have finished my course, I have kept the faith." Not, "I've made a lot of money and I've got a lot of friends and I've got on in life." God is interested in those that finish the course. I meet so many people who have done none of those three things. They are not fighting hard; they are fighting a losing battle! They don't finish their course – they go so far and then they seem to slip up. Many people were in church years ago, maybe went through a Sunday school, made a profession of faith, perhaps were even baptised, but did not finish the course. I even meet ministers who say, "I used to believe what you do when I was a young man, but I've got beyond it now. I've learned so much more." They think they have got beyond the Bible, grown up above it. You find that many ministers set out with a simple faith in the Word of God at the beginning of their ministry, got a bit learned, a bit academic, began to play to the gallery and did not keep the faith.

But Paul is telling Timothy he had done all three things, and for that reason there is a crown waiting, laid up for him, kept safely for him – the crown that is given to those who win. When an athlete finished the course a laurel wreath was placed upon his brow. It faded after three or four days. Paul says, "There's an unfading wreath for you." The word he uses is "wreath" rather than "crown". Being crowned with the victor's wreath was the proudest moment, like a gold medal for an Olympic athlete. That crown is waiting for everyone who looks for Jesus' appearing – for those who condition all their daily life by his appearing – the one before whom they will stand.

Over twenty people are then mentioned: Demas, the man who loved the comfort, ease and prosperity of the world so much that he left Paul. Crescens, Titus, Luke. Paul had a thorn in the flesh, a physical handicap, and the Lord gave him a personal doctor to accompany him on his travels. Isn't that a lovely thought? Mark, the boy who turned back in Acts 13 and was a coward but now he must have improved. Paul says, "Bring him along." Tychicus, Paul's postman who carried the letters to Colossae and to Ephesus. Carpus in Troas, Alexander, a coppersmith who betrayed him to the authorities. He informed the Romans and Paul was arrested. There were: Priscilla and Aquila, husband and wife; Onesiphorus, mentioned earlier in this letter; Erastus, the messenger to Macedonia; Trophimus, Eubulis; Pudens, a Roman soldier who came to Britain, who was stationed near St. Albans and fell in love with a British princess called Claudia. They went back to Rome and both became Christians. There is Lilus, later bishop of Rome.

"Timothy, come to me, and when you come bring my cloak, I'm chilly. Come to me before winter. Bring my cloak and bring the parchments." I think that doesn't refer to his legal documents (his birth certificate and Roman citizenship), but the Old Testament scriptures. Fifteen hundred years later, William Tyndale was in prison for translating scripture into English. He wrote a letter: "Send me, for Jesus' sake, a warmer cap, something to patch my leggings, a woollen shirt, and above all, my Hebrew Bible. Doesn't history seem to repeat itself?

In vv. 17–18 Paul, describing his first trial at which he was released in spite of the fact that he had no counsel for the defence, now looks forward to his coming execution at his second trial. The words he uses are from a Psalm. Five times he almost quotes from Psalm 22, the psalm in our Lord's mind as he died. Look at vv. 16–18. The psalm has, "Why have you forsaken me?" Here Paul says that all forsook him. Psalm 22 has: "There is none to help". Here: "no-one was there to stand by me" Psalm 22, "All the ends of the earth shall turn to the Lord." Here: "That the Gentiles might hear it." Psalm 22: "The kingdom is the Lord's." Here, "He will save me for his heavenly kingdom." This psalm was obviously in the mind of Paul when he died. The scriptures link up beautifully. So the Lord rescued his servant Paul from all evil. Even though he was beheaded, the Lord rescued him through death.

One day, I am looking forward to meeting Paul – not nearly as much as I am looking forward to meeting the Lord, but I want to thank Paul in the name of the Lord for writing these things down, for sharing with us his secrets. The Lord rescues from all evil. You will suffer, but he rescues. The Lord equips you for every good work as you study the inspired word. That is why believers meet together. The Lord judges you for what you have said to other people, as to whether you thought more of what he wants you to say or of what they want you to say. The Lord rewards those who have finished the course, kept the faith and know that there is a crown of righteousness laid up for them. May God apply the scripture to our hearts very deeply.

Read Titus

INTRODUCTION:
    i. From Paul
    ii. To Titus

A. ELDERSHIP (1:15–16)
  1. Appointed (5)
  2. Qualified (6–9)
    a. Domestically secure
    b. Distinctively self-controlled
    c. Doctrinally sound
  3. Heeded (10–16)
    a. Cretan laziness
    b. Jewish legends
    c. Corrupt living

B. MEMBERSHIP (2:1–15)
  1. Instructed (1)
  2. Related (2–10)
    a. Older men and women
    b. Younger men and women
    c. Slaves and masters
  3. Matured
    a. Enabling grace
    b. Awaiting glory
    c. Doing good

C. CITIZENSHIP (3:1–11)
    1. Reminded (1–2)
    2. Saved (3–8)
        a. Past – enslavement and envy
        b. Present – rebirth and renewal
        c. Future – heirs and hope
    3. Protected (9–11)
        a. Foolish controversies
        b. Legalistic arguments
        c. Divisive persons

CONCLUSION:
        i. Doing
        ii. Greeting

By way of introduction we shall look at three things about the letter to Titus. First of all, the people concerned in it; secondly, the place to which it was written, which is very important in understanding the letter; and, thirdly, the purpose for which this letter was written, and that is the most important thing of all.

Titus Chapter 1

I remind you of the two descriptions Paul applies to himself: a "servant" or slave, and an "apostle" or ambassador. Only a Christian would dare to take such words, put them together and apply them to himself. As we have seen, that first word "servant" literally means a slave, someone who is bought by another, owned by another, at the complete disposal of another, and Paul said: "I am a slave of God."

In the Roman Empire the lowest rung of the social ladder was the slave. But in Crete, to which he was writing, part of that great empire, the highest person on the social scale was the ambassador, the envoy of the emperor, the sent one, the apostle, and the word "apostle" comes from a Greek word *apostolos* meaning, "I send". Think of that – Paul is saying that he is the bottom of the social ladder, a slave, but of God; and at the top of the social ladder, an ambassador, a sent one, an apostle, a missionary of Jesus Christ. In a sense this shows you that the Christian has a concern for the whole of society. As Paul says in his testimony in Acts 26, he witnessed to both great and small, to ambassador and slave. He himself was both – a strange mixture, yet you as a Christian are a slave and an ambassador, and that gives you a concern for everybody, whatever level of society they think they belong to. You have a concern, and it is wonderful that

THE PERSONAL LETTERS

in the Christian faith and in the fellowship of a church, social distinctions vanish. We are all slaves, we are all ambassadors. I am not implying that Paul was not an apostle in the special sense. He was, he was sent by the risen Jesus, which we are not – we are sent by the Holy Spirit.

Who was Titus? What was he like? We know very little about him. He is mentioned thirteen times in the New Testament, mostly in the letters and Acts. I think the best way to introduce you to him is to draw a contrast between Titus and Timothy. If Timothy was rather timid by nature, Titus was bold. If Timothy was reluctant to take the lead, Titus was very good at taking the lead. When we study his previous activity, we find that Paul chose Titus whenever he had a difficult and delicate mission to be performed. There are two in particular. There was the big controversy as to whether a Christian should be circumcised. Paul went to Jerusalem to fight it out. He took with him Titus, a Greek, born of Greek parents, not circumcised, to test the church of Jerusalem to see if they would refuse him fellowship on this ground. Now he would only take someone who could stand such a situation, someone who was prepared to be a test case; someone who was prepared to be looked at and discussed and thought over, and Paul took Titus. We know the outcome of that, and the outcome of it is that we do not circumcise Christians today. We have liberty from that. The other situation was Corinth – a very difficult church. It was full of cliques, it had a particularly bad case of immorality in it; their worship was so distorted that people were becoming gluttons and even drunkards at the Lord's Table. Paul sent Titus into that difficult situation to sort it out. In his second letter to Corinth he said, "I'm so glad to hear the good news from Titus that you have begun to put these things right." Now in Crete a difficult situation had also arisen. Paul had to leave. This was after he had been in prison the first time and had been released. Paul had obviously visited Crete and he had visited with Titus, and had left Titus there to sort out the troubles that were developing within the church or the churches.

That brings us to the place. What sort of a place was Crete? It is a long, oblong island south of Greece, as you probably know. It was densely populated. Too many people crowded onto that little island so that Homer the Greek philosopher called it the island of a hundred cities. The population was expanding so much that from time to time the Cretans migrated to other parts of the Mediterranean. Can you think of one well-known tribe or people in the Old Testament who emigrated from Crete? It was the Philistines. They were not native to the Holy Land at the eastern end of the Mediterranean. Amos says, "The Lord brought you from Caphtor" – Crete. The Philistines were simply an overspill from this little island.

Let us look at the character of the Cretans. They had the worst reputation for character of anybody in the ancient world. So much so that the Greek language had a verb, "to cret-ise", which meant to cheat, to lie, to deceive. The Cretans were notorious for their lack of morals – not so much in sexual matters but in matters of honesty and integrity. The Cretan was a man who was a liar and you knew it. You wouldn't trust him. Cicero said that "only the people of Crete consider highway robbery an honourable profession." Philibus said, "They are the only ones in whose estimate no profit is ever disgraceful" – meaning that they didn't mind how they made their money; as long as you made it you were a good man and you were looked up to even if you stooped to the most awful means to get it. Plato said, "They were devoted to money as bees to a honeycomb." I think that is giving you the picture.

At 1:12 Paul quotes a pagan prophet of Crete saying that

Cretans are always liars, evil beasts, and lazy gluttons. That was said six hundred years before Christ.

Now imagine trying to start and build a church in such a community, filling your church with members who in their daily life had been dishonest liars and cheats and were lazy, gluttons, and cruel, evil beasts. Some people say you can't build a church in that sort of situation but that you have got to get to a respectable area then you can build a church. But this is where Paul and Titus went, and they started churches in every town in Crete. But you can see it would raise problems. We are going to study the problems. That, then, is the background. Some have said Paul was a bit tactless in quoting that proverb in that letter, but remember that he was not writing to the churches but to Titus.

It is very important for a minister or a pastor or elders to know what sort of character the people have in the community. Sometimes we hide this from ourselves and we live in a fool's paradise. We refuse to face the facts of what people are really like. But we have got to know so that these things don't creep over into the church of Christ.

Now to the purpose of the letter: why did Paul write? Again the best way to find out is to look for the keywords. If you have a Bible that you don't mind writing on, pull your pencil or pen out and underline some words. This will help you to see what it is all about.

The first keyword that occurs six times (twice in each of the three chapters) is the word *Saviour*. More than in any other letter of Paul, we find that word. The end of v. 3: "God our Saviour...." At the end of v. 4: "Christ Jesus our Saviour". At 2:10, "God our Saviour". The end of v. 13, "... our great God and Saviour Jesus Christ." At 3:4, "God our Saviour", and at the end of v. 6: "Jesus Christ our Saviour." Did you notice something there? In each chapter the first time "Saviour" is applied to the Father and in the second time it is applied to the Son. This is unusual in the Bible. Normally when we speak of the "Saviour" we refer to the Son, and if I say to you, "Do you know the Saviour?" I think you would think of Jesus. But the Bible refers to God as Saviour as well as Jesus Christ. God is the Saviour. He sent Jesus to save us, so this is the first keyword—*Saviour*.

Now there are two other keywords that introduce us to the letter. One is the word "doctrine" and the other is the word "deed" or "deeds". Let us underline these: the first is in v. 9, about halfway through instruction in sound doctrine. Then in v. 16 you have the word "deeds" and the word "deed". At 2:1, "As for you, teach what befits sound doctrine" – note that there is doctrine. In v. 7, "Show yourself in all respects a model of good deeds." In v. 10 we have doctrine again. In v. 14: "good deeds". At 3:8, "... those who have believed in God should be careful to apply themselves to good deeds." And at 3:14, "Let our people learn to apply themselves to good deeds."

Here we have got the theme – if Christ is your Saviour, then two things follow from that: first, sound doctrine; second, good deeds. These two go together, they belong to each other. Most people would agree that Christianity is concerned with good deeds. But a lot of people seek to do some good deeds, whether they are Christians or not. There is more to working out your salvation than doing good deeds. The other side is sound doctrine. These are the two things that we follow after, once we know God and Jesus Christ as our Saviour. So we are concerned with both sound doctrine and good deeds.

Some people think that these two things have no connection, but they have. If your beliefs are not sound, your behaviour will not ultimately be good. If your creed is not what it ought to be, your conduct will not be what it ought to be. Belief affects behaviour, creed affects conduct, doctrine affects deeds. I could take you to family after family where the grandparents or the great-grandparents followed after sound doctrine and therefore produced good deeds, then the parents ignored sound doctrine but managed to keep something of the good deeds, but where the third generation—the children or the grandchildren, have neither sound doctrine nor good deeds. Lose the first and you will lose the second. That is the point of gathering Sunday by Sunday to study the Word.

If a pastor tries to teach sound doctrine, the purpose of doing that is so that from Monday to Saturday the people may adorn that doctrine with good deeds. Indeed if you don't adorn it with that, people won't listen to the sound doctrine. They will say: "Well, if a person goes and listens to all that on Sunday and behaves like that on Monday, I'm not interested."

Now the whole of the letter of Titus is concerned with sound doctrine leading to good deeds. In chapter 1, sound doctrine leading to good deeds in the church; in chapter 2, sound doctrine leading to good deeds in the home; in chapter 3, sound doctrine leading to good deeds in the community at your daily work. You have got the whole letter in a nutshell.

In each of these three chapters (and you can mark it in your Bible), the first few verses are concerned with doctrine, and the next verses with deeds. It is one of the clearest outlines of any book in the New Testament: three points, each with two subdivisions. If you think it is a little mechanical to write out an outline, you can see that Paul had a sort of outline too.

Let us now look at vv. 1–4 in a little more detail. Here are three points: faith, truth and hope, in fact, truth is what we work out in love, and Paul is really thinking here of his old set of three: faith, love, and hope, faith that looks to the past, truth that is worked out in love in the present, and hope that looks to the future. To be set free from the penalty of sin in the past by faith, to be set free from the power of sin in the present by truth in love, and to be set free from the presence of sin in the future – that is our hope. All salvation is included in this. He makes one or two points about these three.

Faith has a human and a divine aspect. It is furthered or fostered by man as he preaches, yet it is ordained by God. I cannot explain this mystery, I only know that, as I preach the Word of God, in some hearts faith is being kindled and furthered and fostered. Yet I know, too, that it is God who is making that happen in that person's heart. I can only stand amazed at this and say, "They are God's elect." I do not understand more than that. I know that when we respond to Christ he says to us, "You did not choose me, I chose you." I stand amazed at such love and grace. Paul, a slave and an apostle to further the faith of God's elect—that is faith. Second: truth. Now with truth you need two things. Truth needs to be *learned* and then it needs to be *lived*, and truth has a double aspect. We *do* it; we don't just hear it. Christians hear teaching in order that they may come to a knowledge of the truth and then work it out in godliness. You learn it first; you live it second. We can, of course, preach what we do not practise – and we are then living a lie, we are contradicting ourselves.

What is our *hope*? This word has lost its meaning. If I say, "I hope so" it means: "I am not very sure but I would like to think it is going to happen." But hope in the Bible means I am absolutely sure. Hope means it is as certain of the future as faith is of the past. I am as certain of my hope, then, as I am of Christ's death for me. What makes that hope certain? First it was *promised*. What a lovely little phrase is inserted here. Remember that Paul is thinking of Crete and he says, "God who never lies...."

Thank God that we worship him, the One who never lies. Plenty of other gods do. If you read the myths about ancient

Greek gods – they lied, they deceived. But we worship God who never lies. We take that for granted. We tell lies ourselves but we never for one moment think that God would tell a lie. We have realised his honesty. It is an aspect of his holiness. God, who never lies, promised eternal life to us. (See 1:2.) If I say I am sure that I have eternal life, it is not because I am sure of *myself* but because God never lies. It is not because I am thinking I am better than anyone else, it is because God promised eternal life, and now it has been preached by Paul in the proper time. Paul says that God promised it ages ago, before time began.

We have missed out a lot of words: grace, peace and others. But we encountered these when we looked at 1 Timothy. In v. 5, Titus is told to do two things: *amend* and *appoint*. "This is why I left you in Crete that you might amend what was defective and appoint elders in every town" – and the rest of the chapter is concerned with the two things. Verse 6a concerns the amending, and vv. 6b–16 the appointing. But it is interesting also that vv. 6–9 talk of doctrine and vv. 10–16 talk of deeds. So you have the same pattern developing again.

Now we look at the appointing. Paul has obviously been in Crete with Titus. They have gone from town to town on that crowded island, preaching the gospel, and everywhere they have gone, people have believed. They have left behind little groups of Christians worshipping God through our Lord Jesus Christ, breaking bread together, baptising one another, hearing the Word of God, serving one another, witnessing to the world.

But there is one thing missing. Those little groups of Christians have no elders, no spiritual leaders. Without these people they are wide open to wrong influences, as we shall see. The cure for false leaders is good leaders. This was very important, yet Paul had not appointed elders for them.

Why not? Because this is something you must never do in a hurry but with time and understanding. So Paul would either wait for twelve months and go back to a church and then say, "Now he is obviously qualified to be an elder," or would send someone else. He might say: Titus, I want you to stay in Crete until each of those churches has its own elders. Then you can leave them. They have got their leadership. We must nurse them until they are ready.

This is the pattern of missionary work. A missionary who goes to a place should preach until there are believers, should gather them in worship and fellowship for the breaking of bread and the prayers, but as soon as is possible should appoint elders. Then the missionary should move on. That is the scriptural pattern and the elders should take over and lead the flock.

We notice a number of things about this. First of all, there were to be elders or bishops – the same word is used here and it means exactly the same. "Elder" refers to their maturity, "bishop" to their ministry. If there were going to be bishops there must be bishops in every place. Paul never for one moment contemplated a bishop of Crete. He said you must appoint bishops, elders in each locality. I want you to notice that he said you must appoint more than one in each place. Not that you must appoint an elder, a pastor, a minister, but you must appoint elders in every place to lead the church. God did not intend any church to be a one-man show.

Then I want you to notice that Paul said as I *directed* you. Not as I *advised* you or not this is one possible pattern. It is an apostolic command.

Now we look at the qualifications listed here and many of them are much the same as 1 Timothy 3, so we can just glance at them. There are three types of qualifications needed here and we label them *domestic* – mainly his qualifications within the home and family life; secondly his *diplomatic* qualifications—his relationships with other people, the matter of friendliness; and, thirdly, his *doctrinal* qualifications in relationship to the faith. These are the three things that you look for in an elder.

First of all, in his family life certain negative things are mentioned. On the negative side, he must be blameless and there is that condition about his marriage. But now is added something more about his children. His children (assuming that they are old enough to be such) must be believers. In other words, if an elder, a man who has the most opportunity with his own children, cannot lead them to the faith, then is he likely to be of help to the family of God? No.

The first test of a man is how far he is able to be a minister to his own family. If he can be a faithful minister there, then he will be able to be a faithful minister in church. It would be quite wrong to call someone to be an elder whose own home and family denied his ability to pass on the faith. For, after all, in church you only see a person for a short time each week. In the home you see them all the time. You have got ample opportunity to talk of the things of God.

Furthermore, two negative things are said about the children: that they must not be open to the charge of being profligate or insubordinate. What do these mean? The word "profligate" is an unfortunate word. It implies certain things but the literal Greek word means unable to save – someone who as soon as they get money spends it; someone who is wasteful and extravagant; someone who has never been taught the value of things and how to use money. It is the same word used in Luke 15: "... and he wasted his money, his substance in riotous, profligate living." In other words, he just went through his money like that. If a man cannot teach his children how to use their money, then he ought not to be an elder.

The other word is "insubordinate". If a man has children

who are rebellious, children who tell him what to do, and who will not be told, then how will he ever rule the household of God? That is the domestic qualification that implies that an elder spends time with his family.

Secondly, there are the diplomatic qualifications of an elder. He is described here as a steward, a man who must manage a household and look after someone else's property. He is God's steward looking after the household of God, the business of God, and therefore he must have certain things. Again on the negative side—what he must not be. He must not be arrogant, self-willed, pleasing himself. He must not be quick tempered or resentful. He must not be a drunkard. He must not be violent, which means literally, a striker. I don't think you would elect an elder who was one who argued with his fists – but just a moment, the word means violent in *speech* as well as with body. We have a word "browbeat." To browbeat a man is to be violent with him, not with your fists but with your words. He must not be a browbeater, not violent and not greedy. The word means someone who literally doesn't care how he makes his money as long as he makes it. Paul is saying that Crete was full of people who did not mind how they made their money. You must never appoint as an elder a man who for base gain will do anything like that. But on the positive side (v. 8) some lovely qualities are here before us: hospitable – literally a lover of strangers, a lover of good. We are not sure if it means good things, good people or good actions. If you have got a man who is a lover of good you have got a lovely man. He is to be master of himself – upright, which means straight; honest, God's plumb line. Do you remember the prophecy of Amos, when he saw God with a plumb line in his hand? A plumb line can only measure one thing. It can't measure size, it can't measure length or depth or breadth. It can only measure uprightness, and that is really the only measure that God has. He doesn't measure how big a person is or how long he lives, he puts the plumb line against a man and says, "Is he upright?" An elder needs to be: "holy and self-controlled" – not unusual or exceptional qualities, but necessary in an elder.

Thirdly *doctrinal*—it is absolutely essential that a man who is going to lead a church and be an elder in it should have a firm grasp not of his own convictions but of the faith once delivered to the saints. He must hold the faith, the sure Word as taught. You can't change the gospel; it is the old, old story. You can put it into new language, you can change the words, but you cannot change the faith, the gospel. An elder must be absolutely reliable here, otherwise he will not be able to do two things. On the positive side, he won't be able to instruct others. That doesn't mean getting up in a pulpit, but when a member of a church goes to an elder and says, "Can you help me?" that elder should be able to instruct them in the faith and say, "Well now, here's a word from the Word of God that I think bears on your case and we will help you to see the right way." But the other side of the elder's job is more difficult—to confute those who contradict it. Some church members would be much happier if their pastor were to stick to the positive side of teaching all the time and never touch the negative, presenting the truth but never criticising those who hold other views and never mentioning those who contradict it. But a teacher has a double job – not only to instruct in the sure word as taught but to confute and to show the flock of God where the wolf lies, even if he is in sheep's clothing, and to show the believer where the false doctrine is being taught.

Now verses 10–16. Not only does Titus have to appoint, he has to amend what is defective. Alas, an alarming number of false teachers, those who were teaching untruths, were getting into the church. It is astonishing that this can happen, yet it does. In church after church in this land, false teachers have got in and people have accepted them. They have been interesting, they have sounded convincing, and people have swallowed it – hook, line and sinker. Nine out of ten churches in this land never touch on the vengeance and the wrath of God. It is right through the Bible and there is more about it in the New Testament than the Old, yet you never hear it. There was not a hymn in the Baptist hymnbook on the subject. Why? Why is it that people have fallen for this? Why is it that they have cut out from their thinking part of the picture of God and forgotten that he is a God like this? Well, because of what is outlined in vv. 10–16: false teachers who said you don't need to believe this now and that those who do are old-fashioned and obscurantists. It is a very real and serious part of Bible teaching. It is because this has been overlooked that there is no fear of God. You rarely meet fear of God either inside the church or outside – the fear of the Lord that is the beginning of wisdom – because God has been distorted and thought of as a sentimental and indulgent old man.

Look at these false teachers. Their character was not very desirable. They were the worst combination that you could find. They combined Jewish and Cretan weaknesses – that is a dreadful combination. The Cretan with his dishonesty, the Jew with his legalism. Their character is described in few words: "They are deceitful." Maybe not consciously so, maybe not because they thought they were deceiving others, but in fact they were. They were deceiving them with empty talk, futile talk, useless talk – it was just talk, and it was hollow, there was no reality of God in it – disturbing, and particularly from v. 11 we notice that they were upsetting families.

One of the surest signs of false teaching is that it upsets family life. It is bound to. False teaching with its legalism, and we have examples today of this, breaks into family life and families are disturbed. They were doing it for money; it was a career, not a calling. As someone has said, "They were not teaching for what they could put into their hearers, they were teaching for what they could get out of their hearers." A man who has gone so low that he can teach religion for purposes of gain has really sunk so low that he ought to be put out of it straight away.

Then we are given teaching on purity. The Jewish idea was that purity consisted of things outside a person that went in. Jesus taught what liberty brings. I am not going to suggest that Jesus encouraged you not to wash your hands before meals – there is a simple ground of hygiene for that – but not to think because you have got washed hands that you are pure; not to think that because you have got Sunday clothes on that you are holy. Jesus said, "It is not what goes into a man that makes him dirty, for that goes simply straight through his body and out. It is what comes out of a man that makes him dirty, out of his heart." To the pure all things are pure. I knew of a girl who spent almost every night in a nightclub in London. But she was not worldly, she was holy; a Salvation Army member, she would go in, trying to preach the gospel in a very difficult place. Some people might have said she was worldly, going into a place like that, but worldliness is not in places, it is in people. I have met people who would never dream of going to such places who are thoroughly worldly inside their hearts. "To the pure all things are pure," says Paul. To be defiled is not outward, it is inward. If your mind and conscience are dirty then you are dirty. If they are clean it doesn't matter where you are, you are pure.

The Jewish idea is here contradicted. Purity is not a matter of washing your hands or where you go. Purity is a matter of having a pure heart. Blessed are the pure in heart for they shall see God. It is a revolutionary concept. If Christians grasp that holiness is inward and not outward, and that purity is of the heart and mind, then they have begun to discover God's will.

In 1:13 Paul speaks of those who are disobedient because their minds and consciences are corrupted, even though they claim to know God. Because they had all these rules they thought they were obeying God. Paul pointed out that they don't know God, they deny him by their deeds. They are unfit for any good deed. Good deeds are a part of a godly life but you can be unfit to do any because you are impure inside. Such people who teach these things must be corrected, and the strong language used is strong medicine for a dreadful disease. First they must be silenced – muzzled. It has become popular now to say "Let's hear all the points of view. Let's hear everybody and put them—all the different views – together and get the truth that way." But we cannot stand poison in the household of God. If a man is teaching this sort of thing then away with him, he must be silenced, muzzled – gagged is the word. He must be gagged.

Therefore, says Paul, rebuke them sharply that they may be sound in the faith. Deal with it. It may need a surgeon's knife, but cut it out for the health of the body of Christ. Now we have seen how to work out doctrine and deeds in the church: firstly, make sure that you have got sound doctrine in the church, and for that you need good elders who are sound in the doctrine themselves; secondly, see that the sound doctrine is adorned with good deeds in the church, so that people hearing the teaching are becoming fit for good deeds. Our relationship to God comes before our relationship to our neighbour and our sound doctrine of him comes before our good deeds to other people.

Titus Chapter 2

So sound doctrine and good deeds belong together. The whole of the Bible puts them together. In most of the letters of the New Testament, the first half of the letter is concerned with doctrine and the second half with deeds. Paul's letter to the Ephesians is a perfect example. Chapters 1–3 are concerned with doctrine; chapters 4–6 are concerned with deeds, and these two must be partners.

The relation between sound doctrine and good deeds needs to be seen in the home. For if Christianity doesn't work out there, then it is not working out at all. Sometimes it is in your own home that it is more difficult to be a Christian than anywhere else, because your family know you best. They know your faults and failings, and you can't keep up a facade for too long within the home. Therefore it is there that a person's good deeds must first of all work themselves out, in the place where we are loved the most in spite of being known the best. That is where Christianity begins, like charity. Chapter 2 begins with a most important word of three letters: "But". Whenever the word "but" occurs in the Bible you must read all the verses before, because what follows that word is a contradiction of what goes before it. When we look at the last few verses of chapter 1, you remember, we find false teachers who are upsetting whole families. False teaching invariably disrupts the home. But true teaching makes home life sweeter, healthier and happier, and altogether more like the pattern that God meant it to be.

Therefore Paul is saying to Titus: "But as for you, teach in such a way that the home and family benefit." You teach what helps whole families and doesn't upset them. You teach the sort of thing that is going to uphold family life and home relationships. That is the subject for this whole chapter. In the first part of it, vv. 1–10, we have a list of the good deeds in the home that befit sound doctrine. In other words, there is not much use in coming to church, hearing sound doctrine and accepting it, and saying, "I'm thoroughly sound in all my views" if, when you get home, the good deeds listed here don't follow. This is what befits sound doctrine in the home and family.

We are taught here, first of all, what those good deeds are that befit sound doctrine in the home as related to older men, older women, younger women, younger men and, finally, slaves. Of course you must bear in mind that behind this writing is the picture of a home in those days and there were very few homes without slaves. The word "household" in scripture does not mean "family" as we mean that. The word "household" in the Bible means, essentially, those who live there, including the slaves and domestic staff. Where you get the baptism of a household it includes the slaves, the staff.

First of all, then, how are older men to behave? The answer can be summed up in one sentence: they are not to behave as younger men. There are certain things that an older man should have left behind. I heard it said of a man well on into his sixties: "You know, he's never grown up. When you know him well, he is like a little child; he is childish in the home – his reactions, his irritability, his temper." Now Paul is saying here that older men should show that they have benefitted from their years of experience, that they have grown up, that they are mature, and therefore different from the younger men.

Here are some of the things that you would expect an older man to have learned. First of all, to have learned to be *temperate* or moderate. Not to be sowing his wild oats. We still have the expression: a man's second childhood. A man should never get into his second childhood. He should remain in his manhood and stay right there. Alas, that does not always happen. "Temperate" originally referred to wine or strong drink but it never meant total abstinence. To be temperate is to know when to stop. A man who is older should have learned when to stop. He should be self-controlled. But the word "temperate" also applies to everything else. An older man should be self-controlled.

Secondly, an older man should be *serious*. There is something rather degrading about an older man who is silly. It does not mean gloomy or being a kill-joy, but it does mean that he has been around so many corners in life that he realises life is a serious business, and that the nearer he gets to the end of it the more serious it does become, and he takes life seriously. It does not mean that he lacks a sense of humour or that he cannot laugh or smile. But it does mean that he is serious in his attitude to life and not flippant or silly.

Thirdly, he is to be *sensible* and this means someone who is not rash or reckless. Some young men are reckless, rash and rush in where angels fear to tread. Don't expect old heads on young shoulders.

One of the biggest difficulties in a church is that the older members expect the younger men to be temperate, serious, and sensible. When you do find that, it is such an outstanding thing that the whole church notices it. But don't normally expect younger men to be like this. This comes with the years. You must not expect a young man who is newly converted to be completely sensible and to be always serious. He will learn and develop, but often tension develops between older men and younger men in a church because the older men are expecting the younger men to behave as themselves. Again, elders need to have real understanding at this point or elders by their very age could become impatient with youth.

Then you would expect an older man to be sound in faith and in love and in steadfastness – that he has held on to these three things and grown in them. His love is not to be mere sentimentality. His steadfastness is not to be mere obstinacy. An older man can be terribly obstinate but that is not steadfastness, not sound, it is most unhealthy. So you look for these things. Youth may be unstable, intemperate, unthinking. We should expect older men to have matured and grown up.

Secondly, there are the older women (v. 3ff.). The first phrase is a most interesting one in the original language – "reverent in behaviour". I don't think the translators would dare to translate the original word. It says they should behave like "priestesses". Now we believe in the priesthood of all believers. That means I am a priest. Don't take that out of context – I am a priest, but so is every Christian. We are a kingdom – a race – of priests, and that means that the ladies are priestesses. In the ancient world they had priestesses in the temples. Of them was expected a certain standard of behaviour. Here the older women are told to behave as priestesses, as holy women of God wherever they are. In a very real sense, a godly woman is a priestess in the home as a godly man is a priest in the home, mediating the grace of God to others within that family.

As well as the reverence that belongs to such a sacred calling, the older women are not to be slanderers – and we seem to come down to earth with a bump. We have seen this again and again, but it is clearly one of the dangers for women who grow older that they become gossips and slanderers and they are not to be that. Coupled with that is slavery to drink. That is perhaps not so common, though it is often the case of those who are trying to forget, trying to escape, trying to forget that they are older than they were – those who have not learned to grow old gracefully and to accept the passing years as a maturing of God (or, as the crude phrase puts it, are trying to be mutton dressed up as lamb). Such people may turn to drink as the way to forget. It is one of the ways out of that looking back attitude which so often comes and which there is no need to have. Thirdly, they are to teach what is good, and we will come back to that.

Then we turn to the younger women. What is to be said to the younger women? It assumes that they are married here. First of all, they are to love their husbands and children. I want you to notice that love is something that can be *trained*. The modern conception of love is that you either have it or you haven't; that you fall into it or you fall out of it. It is something that is just there, and that is it. That modern concept of love is not the biblical concept. Love is something that you are trained in. Now if love is something that just happens, something that you just fall into, you either love or you don't, then how can you ever say to someone, "You shall love the Lord your God," or "You shall love your neighbour"? If it is something that happens to you then you cannot do it, it is done to you.

Many marriages today are being built on this concept of love – that it is just something that has happened to you and there is nothing more to it. But a younger woman needs to be trained to love her husband and trained to love her children. There is need for marriage training. We cannot assume that because young women have fallen in love, everything is going to be fine.

Next, they ought to be *sensible* and they are to be chaste, and the reason for that with younger women is obvious. They are to be domestic, literally workers at home. Without going back to that narrow view that a woman ought never to step outside her kitchen door, nevertheless in God's plan this is her first and highest calling. Even if there are political and social and church activities that a wife can engage in, her first calling is to build a home. That is the first calling of a minister's wife – not to be an unpaid curate but to build a home for the minister. It is the first calling of an elder's wife or a deacon's wife – not to be an official of the church but to build a Christian home.

I think many other Christian servants would say that if they had a home in which whenever they came home their wife was out doing something else elsewhere, they could not do what they do for the Lord. The backing of a home in which there is a young wife who has learned to be domestic is one of those blessings that every Christian worker needs. That is her first calling. If she can fit in with that other callings: socially, politically, in the church, and so on, well and good. But there are homes where the wife has done so much of that she has not been able to be domestic, not been able to look after the family.

Next—*kind*. It is interesting that it follows *domestic* because with all the domestic duties you can become so irritable and so tired that this slips, and it follows from the previous point. It means to be generous and helpful, understanding and sympathetic. Lastly, to be *submissive* to their husbands. This is about as unpopular as some of the other things we have mentioned, yet there it is. God has a pattern for the home, and those who fit into his pattern will find the happiest home. There will not be resentment or difficulty. There will be harmony and partnership, and part of God's teaching is that Christ is the head of the husband and the husband is the head of the wife—that is the pattern. Wherever you have that pattern, I will show you a very happy Christian home where personal relationships fit in with harmony and with peace.

Now the younger men – only one thing is said to them and that is a very important thing. Urge the younger men to control themselves. Youth has certain characteristics. Here youth has confidence but not experience. Youth has education but not wisdom. Youth has strength, far more than many of us have who are older (and we wonder where they get their energy from), but not stability. Lastly, youth has zeal but not knowledge.

Now this is the characteristic of a young man and you see it in young Christians. They have enthusiasm but not the wisdom that keeps it in the right channels. A young person's first job is to master self. If they can learn that, they will be able to master anything else. It is the lesson we need to learn in the late teens and early twenties. Yet so enthusiastic are we, and I can remember this very clearly myself, you are so enthusiastic to master everything and everyone else, and the one thing you don't bother with is mastering yourself. So you want to put the world right and you want to put the church right and you want to put this, that, and the other right. Why don't those old fogies in the church let us put the church right, and why don't they do this, that, and the other. This is characteristic, but I repeat: a young person's first job under God is to master themselves. When they have done that, all their enthusiasm, all their zeal, all their powers, all their strength will be rightly channelled. Urge the young men to master themselves then they will be able to master others, then they will be able to master the situation. That is the one thing for young people. He that rules his spirit, says the book of Proverbs, is greater than he who takes the city. But I think most young people would rather take a city, it is more glamorous.

Now slaves. First, they were to be submissive to their masters, not rebellious. They were to be satisfactory, efficient, even though they were not paid. They must not literally answer back. I do not like the word "refractory" which we don't use much. It literally means talking back. Someone, if he is told to do a thing, talks back, argues. He must be honest, not pilfering, and the slaves used to do that in lieu of wages. They did not get any wages so they pinched whatever they could. Petty pilfering is now a national pastime in this country. We are not to do that but, to be honest, this still applies. Finally, they were to be loyal and faithful.

Who is to do the teaching? Well, in the case of the older women and the younger men and the slaves, Titus is to do the teaching. But I want you to notice one group that he is not to teach: Titus is not to teach the younger women. They are to be taught by the older women. That is very significant and important. The job of teaching younger women in the church and in the home is that of older women. After all, they are the best to do it. Not only does it avoid wrong temptations but it also means that the people who have experienced these things are able to teach them. So that Titus is to teach all the men and the slaves, and he is to bid the older woman how to behave, but he is to leave the teaching of the younger women to older women.

This is one of the reasons for having women's meetings and women's classes in a church. It is more important to have that than groups for men, from this point of view. It provides the conditions in which older women can train and teach younger women so that this is why throughout the church you will find more women's meetings than men's meetings. I think that's probably a right and a proper thing. It provides the situation in which this can be done.

How is it to be taught? What is the method of teaching? Look back at 2:1. The word for "teach" here is not the word used elsewhere for teaching from a pulpit. It is the word, "speak" or in conversation. So Titus is being told: as you go from house to house if you meet an older man tell him this, if you meet a younger man tell him that; you older women, as you meet younger women you tell them this. This is where this sort of teaching is to be given – in the home, in the setting. We don't do as much of this as we should. I confess I don't do it as much as I should.

The saintly Richard Baxter went to Kidderminster as

vicar. When he arrived there was hardly a house that was Christian. When his ministry there was over there was hardly a house that was not Christian. Do you know how he did it? He went from house to house, he went down a road and he said, "Monday morning I'll be going down such and such a street," and he took with him his Bible. He didn't talk about the weather; he didn't talk about anything else. As soon as he got in the house he read a passage from the Bible and taught them in the home the truth, and then he left. He went next door and he asked the whole family to be present when he came. He just did that week in, week out.

Well, how is Titus to teach? Two things – first he is to teach in word and secondly in deed. It is very important that this double teaching should be given. What we say and what we do should balance. If our lips say one thing and our lives say another, no one is going to take any notice.

There are four things that there need to be in his word. Firstly, in v. 7: *integrity*; integrity of speech so that people can rely on what he says. Secondly, *gravity*. He is not to entertain. I do not preach to entertain. You can get cheaper entertainment at home on television. You do not go to church to be entertained. Whether it is interesting or not, we are in church to be edified, built up, taught, and therefore there is to be gravity in our teaching not just a string of stories, even if people like that. Thirdly, *dignity*. Teaching is not to be unsound, unhealthy. And it must be sincere.

Finally, notice in v. 15: with all *authority*. Some people have the impression that a Christian teacher is giving advice and that it is up to you whether you take it or not, but that is not so. A Christian teacher is to teach with all authority and he is not to let anyone who hears him disregard what he says. It applies to the old women too, when they teach. Teach with all authority. You are not giving good advice; you are not saying what might be done. You are saying, "This is what

God tells you to do." Let no one disregard you. Follow it up and people know that this is what the church stands for. This will therefore involve (v. 15) exhorting and reproving. I wish it didn't! It would be much easier not to, but exhorting means to encourage someone and commend them, but to reprove them means to criticise them and indeed to condemn them. It would be much nicer if we could stick to saying, "I exhort you, I encourage you, I commend you for doing this." But the other half of teaching is to say: "I condemn you for doing that. I commend you for doing this; I condemn you for doing that. I exhort you. I reprove you," and to do both with all authority requires great grace. Next (go back to v. 7), a teacher should not only teach in word but in all respects be a model of good deeds. That is not so easy, is it? That is why we hesitate to teach others. That is why an older woman may hesitate to teach a younger woman, knowing that if that younger woman came into her own family she might see that this older woman is not keeping these duties herself. But we are to be a model, a type, a pattern to preach what we practise, to demonstrate what we declare – that is Christian teaching.

Why are we to teach these things? In vv. 1–10 there are three motives given. The first is in v. 5, the second is in v. 8, and the third is in v. 10. The reason is that the world judges our gospel by what we do, not by what we say. We can preach till we are blue in the face, but if our lives do not show the practical effects of what we hear on Sunday, the world will criticise. See v. 5: we are to do this that the Word of God may not be discredited. The trouble is that we believe in the Bible and the world knows we do, and for better or for worse the world will call us Bible-thumpers. They will ridicule this book if our lives don't match up. They will discredit the Word of God if it has no effect on our home life, if they can come into our home and see us behaving in such a way that

God cannot possibly be in it – discrediting the Word of God.

Secondly, in v. 8: "... so that our enemies may be ashamed of themselves." They do look at us. They do criticise us. As soon as they can, they will point a finger at us, but if we are behaving in the right way as set out here they will be ashamed of themselves. Indeed, one of the best testimonies I know is a Christian home. If a man is critical, if a man is against the faith, you get him to go into a Christian home and sooner or later he will come out and say, "There's something in that home that I can find in no other. There is a happiness, a joy, a peace, a harmony – there is a relationship in that home; it is a joy to go into it." So they will be ashamed that they criticised you – that is the second reason.

Thirdly in v. 10: that in everything they may adorn the doctrine. Now the word "adorn" is interesting. It is entirely used in scripture of jewellery. Now the world adorns things with expensive jewellery, but the jewellery that a Christian needs to wear is not very expensive though it is very costly; it is the jewellery that adorns the gospel and makes it attractive to other people, drawing their attention to it. That jewellery is this sort of behaviour in the home. It attracts people; it makes the gospel a thing that they will love. I have heard more than one person who said they were first brought to Christ or brought to consider Christ by the jewellery of good deeds within the home.

I think of a Durham miner who is in heaven now, who had a little council house which had a small front room. Into that house every Sunday came forty-five young people. They crowded in, most of them off the streets. It ruined his furniture, but fortunately his wife was more proud of people than of houses. She was not house-proud in that sense. You could see the poor springs in the sofa; they went after a few weeks. But the people came into that home from godless homes and they saw a grandfather and a father and a mother and a son living the Christian life. Out of that house came ministers and missionaries, and all sorts of other things – it is marvellous. But they were so impressed with the sheer joy of a Christian home where the furnishing came second and where people came first, and where there was an atmosphere of welcome and love and of all that there ought to be. It is such jewellery that the world wants, more than their own sort of jewellery and we ought to adorn the doctrine in this way.

Now we come to the second half of chapter 2, vv. 11–14. Here we have a section that is concerned with the doctrine that lies behind the good deeds we have mentioned. It begins with a little three-letter word "for". If you read the word "but" in the Bible it means that everything that follows the word contradicts what goes before, but if you read the word "for", everything that follows that word confirms what goes before – the word "for" connects it up. Now there are four verses here and I give each of them a little label. They are so full of truth, and they are so straightforward and simple.

First of all you notice that *appearing* occurs twice in vv. 11 and 15: the appearing of his grace and the appearing of his glory. In vv. 11 and 12 the "his" refers to God the Father. In vv. 13 and 14 the word "his" refers to God the Son. The Christian stands between two appearings. The grace of God has appeared; the glory of Christ is going to appear. We stand between those two. We look back to the one, forward to the other. The grace of God has appeared in Jesus. The glory of Christ has yet to appear. Our daily life is always conditioned by these two facts: that the grace has already appeared to us and that the glory is going to. As you go through your daily life Monday to Saturday, these are the two thoughts that will keep you on the straight and narrow path: the grace that has already come and the glory that is going to come. Next we notice that in both cases the appearing implies a certain response in our own life – in the one case godliness;

in the other case goodness. The appearing of the grace of God for the salvation of all people leads to this thought: that salvation had a purpose, on the one hand negative, on the other positive—the negative that we should renounce something and the positive that we should live a life of righteousness. We should renounce irreligion altogether. That is the point of coming to church to worship. We are renouncing irreligion. There will be many irreligious people who will either stay in bed or dig their garden or wash their car or go for a run or sit and read the newspaper. We have renounced irreligion and we are now seeking to live a godly life. We have also renounced worldly passions, which means an inordinate desire for pleasure or for possessions or for power or for any other thing that the world seeks – we have renounced that.

We are now seeking three things positively. Towards ourselves: *sober*. Towards other people: *upright*. Towards God: *godly*. Here is a three-dimensional righteousness. When the grace of God appeared for our salvation, the purpose of it was that we should renounce what is wrong and walk in righteousness. Insofar as the grace of God has appeared for our salvation and has not led to this, there has been a failure. From time to time one hears parents say to a child, "After all I've done for you, this is how you behave; this is how you show your gratitude?" Well, God could say that to me and to every one of us: After all I've done for you, you won't renounce this and you won't walk that way.

The grace of God has appeared for this, but our hope is related to our holiness. If we had a more lively sense of the return of our Lord Jesus we should live holier lives, living a good life in this world because we are awaiting our blessed hope, and as you look forward and realise that when Jesus comes back he is going to ask you how you have spent your money, how you have spent your time, how you have used your gifts, how you have walked in this world, this is a tremendous stimulus to holiness. We need to realise that when he looks at you he will see everything. I think the eyes of Jesus are both wonderful and dreadful at the same time. They were enough to break Peter's heart. He just turned and looked at Peter, and one day the eyes of Jesus are going to look at you physically – you will see that.

When you have realised that, it keeps you in the straight and narrow way. You see things in the right perspective. That great social reformer Lord Shaftesbury, do you know why he did what he did? Do you know why he got the children out of the mines and the factories? If ever you saw his notepaper you would see, because printed at the top it said this: "Even so, come Lord Jesus." When you know that he is coming, you get on with the work here. So those who say that people who talk of the second coming and who think about nothing but the second coming are no use in this world, read the life of Lord Shaftesbury! It is those who really have their eyes fixed on the blessed hope who really live godly lives right here: useful, upright and honest lives.

Now look at the end of v. 13, about which there has been a lot of controversy. I want to show you something very important because next time a Jehovah's Witness calls at your door I want you to show them this verse. Mind you, they will argue and they'll try and get around what I am going to explain. But if you stand firm on this verse, they will go away and they won't trouble you again. There are two possible translations: "The glory of our great God; and our Saviour Jesus Christ," or, "The glory of our great God and Saviour Jesus Christ." The question is: is the Word of God here referring to Jesus or to his Father? If it is referring to our Lord Jesus, then Jehovah's Witnesses fall completely to the ground. Their whole belief cracks because they will not accept that Jesus is God. Neither will the Mormons, neither will the Spiritualists, neither will the Christian Scientists. You will find that all these people have this in common. They will not use the word "God" of Jesus. But our claim and our understanding is that in fact this word "God" is used of Jesus in the Bible. Said Thomas, "My Lord and my God." Here says Paul writing to Titus, "Our God and Saviour." You will notice if you have a Bible with marginal notes that there is an alternative translation to this verse, which separates God from Saviour and only applies the second to Jesus. Well, let us look at that.

First of all, do you remember that both in chapter 1 and in chapter 3 the word "Saviour" is applied twice – once to God the Father and once to God the Son? In 1:3, "God our Saviour"; in 1:4 verse four, "Jesus our Saviour"; in 3:4, "God our Saviour"; in 3:5, "Jesus our Saviour". Now go back to 2:10, "God our Saviour"; end of v. 13, "Saviour, Jesus Christ". Therefore we have established first that Jesus is the main person referred to here. Secondly, it is grammatically correct to apply "God" to Jesus Christ in this passage. If it was going to be two persons it would have said in the original language, "the glory of the great God and the Saviour Jesus Christ". But the second "the" is missing, which means that the two words were applied to exactly the same person. It is our God and Saviour Jesus Christ. Not God and the Saviour, but our *God and Saviour Jesus Christ*. There are many other reasons I could give you. One is that this word, "appearing" is never applied to God the Father in the Bible but only to God the Son, the appearing of the great God and Saviour Jesus Christ. In other words, here we have a statement in the Word of God specifically to the effect that Jesus is God. When your Jehovah's Witness calls, take him to this verse and say, "There, my Bible says that Jesus is God. Do you believe that? If you don't, then we don't have the same faith." It is the one thing that he cannot accept: that Jesus is the *God and Saviour* Jesus Christ.

In v. 14 we turn to the purpose of his sacrifice. Why did Jesus die? What was the cross all about? We notice that he died to *redeem us from* something and to *purify us for* something. We often forget that salvation is both. We are not only saved *from* but *to*. He is able to save, redeem, rescue, from all iniquity. That is the "from" side but there's another side. It is God's intention through Jesus Christ to have a people that belong to him for one purpose: that they might be zealous for good deeds.

We should be zealous for good deeds. Multiply that by infinity and you have got God's purpose. God's purpose was to have a group of people on earth who were zealous for good deeds, and that is why he sent Christ to die. To save us from sin is half the battle, it was also to save us for good deeds, and in a very real sense good deeds are a vital part of salvation – that he might purify for himself a people of his own that he could use on earth. The old poem "Christ has no hands but our hands" applies here. He has chosen to have a people through whom he works on earth.

Titus Chapter 3

As we have now seen, the whole theme of the letter is the relationship between sound doctrine and good deeds, the partners of the Christian faith: what we believe and how we behave; our creed and our conduct. Therefore all the way through, Paul is instructing Titus: teach them sound doctrine so that they may apply themselves to good deeds. Let these two go together. This is the double testimony, by lip and by life, that the church is meant to make and woe betide our testimony if it is not two-fold.

Some people say, "Well, I just want to witness with my life. I just want to do good deeds." You will never lead a soul to Christ that way. Then there are others who just want to preach and to pass on sound doctrine but are not interested in good deeds. They will never win a soul to Christ that way either. But the person whose lips and whose life are at the disposal of the Lord, and both are giving the same message of the grace and mercy of God, will be a profound influence on their neighbours.

Chapter one was concerned with how we work this out in church, chapter two with how we work it out in the home and family life, and chapter three concerns how we work it out in the community outside. The Christian life, if I can draw a little diagram in your mind, is worked out in a series of circles. The first place we begin to act in a Christian way is within the church. If you don't learn to be a Christian there, you won't learn to be Christian anywhere else. That is the place we are meant to learn. For example, we are told to love our neighbour but if we are going to do that we have got to start by beginning to learn to love our brother, our fellow Christian. If we are going to witness outside, we shall learn to do it by talking about the things of Christ inside where it is much easier, and that is the purpose of holding meetings in church where members can speak and testify to the things of the Lord, so that when they go out from that inner circle, they can go on witnessing. The next circle out is the circle of the home. The Bible says that one believer in a family is enough to sanctify it in the Lord's sight (see 1Corinthians 7) – a believing wife or husband means that in God's sight there is something unique about that family. It is a sanctified unit. One believer in a family circle can make all the difference. Then outside that further still, we learn to be Christians in church, we go home and we practise it there, and we go out to the community where we are the salt of the earth and the light of the world. In our Lord's mind, "salt" was not meant as a flavour or even as a preservative. Those are uses to which we put salt today, but he meant two things. First of all, they used salt as a disinfectant in their rather primitive hygiene arrangements, and they also used it as a fertilizer. It was there to stop bad things from growing; it was there to encourage good things to grow, and we are the salt in the community.

In chapter 3, as in chapters 1 and 2, we begin with the list of good deeds and then we go on to the sound doctrines that lie behind them. Of the good deeds Paul says, "Remind them of these" – which means first of all that he had already told them of these things right from the beginning, but second that it is very easy to forget them, so we need to be reminded of our duty to the community again and again.

There are three groups of people mentioned here to whom, by implication, we are related: firstly, those who are set in authority over us, rulers, those in government; secondly, those for whom we work, and thirdly, our neighbours. Now see what our duties are. The Bible leaves us in no doubt as to our duties towards the state. It is clear from this that a Christian has a duty to support the state financially by paying up all his taxes and not trying to evade a single penny. That is the first thing. Secondly, he has a duty to support them morally by giving respect to those who are set in authority. Their authority depends on the respect in which they are held. We are to support them spiritually by praying for them and morally by doing what they tell us, unless what they tell us is contrary to God's will.

Many years ago I was impressed listening to missionaries who had got out of Congo and were testifying to their experiences. The rebel authorities who had taken over the upper Congo area in which they lived had made them do the most idiotic and silly things, yet they felt that unless any one of them was a compromise of a basic principle, they must show even to those rebels that they were prepared to do what they were told. For example, the rebel would turn up and

THE PERSONAL LETTERS

say, "Give us your Land Rover," and they gave it. The rebels would turn up and tell them to stand outside their homes for hours and they did it. In other words, a Christian should go out of his way to show that he is a law-abiding citizen. The reason for saying this to Titus is obvious. The island of Crete in which Titus then was living, and to which this letter was addressed, was fretting and fuming under the Roman yoke. Constantly the Cretans were organising rebellion and insurrection against the Roman authorities. It would have been absolutely disastrous for the little Christian churches growing up in that place to become associated with political agitation. Paul is telling Titus to teach the believers to be submissive to rulers and authorities, even to the Romans. It was as unpopular advice as the word of our Lord that if a Roman soldier compels you to carry his bag one mile (which he had a legal right to do), you should carry it a second mile.

This is not very popular amongst those who want to stir things up politically, but Christians should not be in the vanguard of political agitation unless they are being told to do something contrary to their faith, when they must say "We must obey God rather than men."

The next thing we are told is in relation to employers. We are to be obedient and ready for any honest work. We have a duty to serve the community, which does so much for us. Somebody has said that the daily work we render is the rent we pay for our room on earth. We ought to make a contribution to the society from which we have reaped so much benefit. Once again, to be told that they must be ready for any honest work would not go down well with the Cretans because, we recall, in 1:12 we learnt that a prophet of Crete said that Cretans are always liars, evil beasts, and lazy gluttons. Lazy people, they were not ready for any honest work. If they could make the money in any other way they did. If they could make it an easy way without working for it they would. Here they are told to be ready for any honest work. A Christian must be one who is ready for work. After all, we were made for work. God is a worker and we are made in his image. Christ said, "My father works until now, and now I work." He called us to work while we still could, before the night comes when no man could work.

In other words, the Bible would see the true meaning of a man's life not in his leisure but in his work – which is a complete reversal of the modern approach to the secret of life which is: your work is a necessary evil to get the money in order to fulfil your life in leisure. You can see the difference of outlook. A Christian is one who is ready for any honest work, and the word "honest" is important here. John Wesley used to say to the early Methodist: you must never take a job which will harm anyone's body, anyone's mind, or anyone's spirit – such would be a dishonourable and a dishonest way for a Christian to get his money. That is a very good summary of honest work. A Christian should not despise manual or menial work if it is rendering a service to the community.

Thirdly – our neighbours. The most important factor in our relationship to our neighbours is our speech about them. Our relationship to neighbour is more dependent on our tongue than on anything else. Indeed, this is why gossip tends to be localised and limited to neighbours. So a Christian will not speak evil behind his neighbour's back and will not speak evil to his face. He will speak evil of no-one and will avoid quarrelling, which is to speak evil to someone's face directly. Slander and gossip are still among the most serious sins of the human race, if you judge sin by the results of such things.

So on the negative side, we are not to speak wrongly either behind a neighbour's back or to a neighbour's face, but we are to behave as true gentlemen and true ladies. What makes a gentleman? That he has aristocratic blood in his veins? Or studied books on etiquette? What makes a true lady? Is it that she went to a finishing school in Switzerland? No, I have known true gentlemen and ladies who have none of these things. One of the truest gentlemen I knew ate his peas off a knife! A gentleman is a gentle man, that is all. He will be courteous towards other people. Courtesy is not etiquette. Sometimes the rules of etiquette leave you so confused you wonder if you will ever make the grade, especially when you are working out all the protocol with the relatives for a wedding reception – where you should sit and so on. It is a dreadful business. Etiquette consists of man-made rules, but courtesy and gentleness are God-given qualities. Both of them are really an expression of love for someone in little things – consideration. To be gentle with somebody is to feel their needs, to feel their situation, and a gentle person is a gentleman – that is the biblical view of etiquette at any rate. We notice that we are to show perfect courtesy toward all people. It is easier to show perfect courtesy to some or imperfect courtesy to all. But the Bible sets the standard as high as it possibly can: perfect courtesy toward all.

To summarise, then, in the community the Christian has to witness in his life – towards his rulers with submission; towards his employers with obedience and readiness for any honest work (and that means, of course, that if it is dishonest he must say, "I'm sorry I can't do it"); and towards his neighbours, not speaking wrongly either behind their backs or to their faces, but rather with a gentleness and a courtesy toward them. Now why should we do these things? We turn now from the good deeds to the sound doctrine, and always behind the deeds lies the doctrine. Why should we behave towards people in this way, whoever they are and whatever they are like? The answer is because we were once like them. We once added problems to life instead of solving them.

One of the things a Christian needs to remember all the time is what he or she used to be like, and it is very difficult to do this. After you have grown up, it is very difficult to imagine what you were like as a child. After you are married, it is very difficult to remember what it was like to be single. After you have taken any step in life it becomes almost impossible to imagine what you were like before you took that step. Above all, after you have become a Christian it is almost impossible to imagine life without Christ. You find it impossible. He has come to mean so much to you, and prayer has come to mean so much to you, and the Word of God has come to mean so much to you, and the church has come to mean so much to you, that you find it almost impossible to understand your neighbour who never opens his Bible and who never gets on his knees except when he is in a jam and who would never dream of coming to church and who is an awfully nice soul and showing no need whatsoever of spiritual help. Therefore it is very difficult to be patient and sympathetic to those in that condition. The best way around it is to remember what you once were – exactly the same. Whitfield saw a criminal going to the gallows and said, "There but for the grace of God, go I" – and this is true. If it were not for the grace of God that came to us through godly parents, through being brought up with Sunday school teaching maybe, for being brought in contact with the true gospel, through having a church to go to where we can get the truth – if it was not for that you would be just the same as your neighbour. You would probably not even be ashamed of it. So we need to remember this. That should not breed pity. In some people that just breeds pity for others. It should breed gratitude to God, that he should take me though I was just the same as my neighbour, and that he should lift me up to there and make me what I am – such grace and such mercy.

We have in vv. 3–7 the two basic doctrines of Christianity. There are only two: sin; salvation. Wesley again used to say: "Know your disease, know your cure." Know what is wrong with you and know how to put it right; know what has gone wrong with the human race and know what God has done to put it right. That is the double knowledge we need. In other words: sin; salvation. So this is the doctrine behind our good deeds: that we were sinners; that we have found salvation.

First of all then, let us look at sin. I have already mentioned seven virtues of the Christian in the first two verses, but now in the third verse there are seven vices. Seven things that were true of every one of us before we knew Christ. If we don't know Christ, they are still true of us. *The first thing is that you are a fool if you don't know Christ.* It is interesting to take the Bible and look through the word "fool". For example, there was a man who said: Now business is good; I am going to expand my business until I have got enough money to retire on and then I'm going to retire and build myself a nice house and enjoy my remaining years. Jesus said: "You fool."

Before you are a Christian you are a fool because you think that money can get you things. You think that if you pull down your barns and build greater you are getting on and that you have got security, but you are foolish and we don't see it. We are fools and we don't know it. Take another mention of the word "fool" in scripture, "The fool has said in his heart there is no God." Now you notice he hasn't said it in his mind. It is in his heart that he said it, which is very different from being an atheist. A man who says there is no God with his mind is an atheist. But a man who says there is no God with his heart is a fool. If you read the context it means this: a man who thinks that he can get away with something and that God will not call him to account for it; a man who does wrong and doesn't have any qualms of conscience and his heart says, "It's alright, God will forgive; God won't do anything about it." That man is a fool. Before we knew Christ we were foolish. We thought we could get away with things. We thought there was to be no day of reckoning, we thought there would be no Day of Judgment, we thought we would never be called to account, and we thought that as long as we could keep our sins hidden and underground that they were forgotten and that they would never be brought up. What fools we were! Foolishness is the first characteristic of sin.

Secondly, *we were disobedient*. The one thing that is true of every human being on earth is if you tell them not to do a thing, they will want to go and do it. I was talking to some young people in a school – the fourth, fifth, and sixth forms. They were trying to convince me that in fact everybody was innocent not guilty before God, and that we were all very nice people really. I told them again of an illustration which is as good as any. I said, "Supposing I put you in a school library with every book on every subject you ever wanted to read all around the walls, and enough books to keep you interested for a lifetime, and put you all in there but left one book on one shelf not to be read by anyone under twenty-one and you are left there. What are you going to do?"

At last they all grinned and virtually admitted by their faces what they would do. Now I said, "Why? You've no need to look at that book. You have got ample books in the library to last you a lifetime – interesting, helpful books. There is only one book that is bad for you to read and it is fortunately labelled so you don't need to read it and yet you will all make a bee line for it. Then I referred them to Genesis 3 and said, "You know this happened right from the beginning. We haven't changed one iota. You can eat of all the trees of the garden but there's just one you can't – not to be touched." Of course this was the one they just had to go for. Then I said, "What's wrong with this? Is it not so that when we are out of Christ there is a streak in us that is disobedient?" If we are told not to do a thing, we immediately want to do it. That is a characteristic of sin. That is why the commandments of God saying "Thou shalt not" appear irksome to the sinner but not to the saint.

Thirdly, when we are in a state of sin we are *easily led astray*. Anybody can twist us. Anybody can convince us. We can read this and that and the other and we will be convinced and the one book that won't convince us is the Bible. Isn't that astonishing? Some "celebrity" just has to say what he thinks about life after death and thousands will be convinced that's right. Even though what is said utterly contradicts the Bible. So easily are people led astray. A scientist pronounces on a miracle and people flock to the viewpoint that he has expressed, even though it contradicts the Bible. They are led astray – not only intellectually, but morally. I can remember well enough the times when I had the wrong sort of companion and was so easily led astray. I have sat in law courts and heard people in the dock say, "I've got into wrong company. They led me astray." But this is a characteristic of sin – that you are led astray by other people and you do things that you never wanted to do yourself. You just do it because the others do it and they lead you.

Fourthly: *slaves to various passions and pleasures*. The two great masters of men according to James 4 are passions and pleasures. Now there is nothing wrong with pleasure in itself. It is when someone becomes a slave to it – for example, when he is possessed by his possessions and he can't say no and he can't stop. He has got to pursue these things and he has become chained in his soul by his own pleasures and passions – that is sin. It is not freedom. A person who says "I want to be free to do what I like" will sooner or later finish up in slavery. In this sort of slavery he will find the chains are there. He will not find them loosed until he can say, "My chains fell off, my heart was free; I rose, went forth and followed thee." It is this sort of chain that grips a man and ties him to his pleasures forever. It is going to be sheer hell when he is in hell without those pleasures yet his soul is still chained to the memory and desire of them.

Fifthly: *passing our days in malice*. This is a stronger word than mischief. It means wanting to do people harm, wanting to take a rise out of them, wanting to answer them back, wanting to be on top of them, wanting to be better than the proverbial "Jones's" and not just keep up with them.

Sixthly: *envy*. That is a horrible thing and yet it can get inside a church. It can get inside a Christian. It can get right inside a saint. It was envy that killed Abel. It was envy that put Joseph in the pit. It was envy that started the first rebellion against Moses and Aaron. It was envy in Saul against David. It was envy in Annas and Caiaphas that put Jesus to death – it is a horrible thing. It really does eat away, and envy is one of the characteristics of sin. You see somebody who has more money than you have or more friends than you have, or more gifts than you have, and one of the things that sin does is to give you a twinge of envy. If there is anybody who is outside of Christ who can say, "I have no trace of that", I would like to meet you. We have all got a trace of that – some more, some less but it is there.

Seventhly (and finally) – *hated by men and hating one another*. Is this true? The word "hated" here means to be loathsome, to be repulsive, to be offensive. It doesn't mean that people will not pretend to like you. It means that, in fact, they just don't like you because they see their own faults in you and you see your faults in them, and so you don't like each other. You can't get on with each other. You find each other basically repulsive, off-putting. That is, of course, the climax of this list.

Now this is what we were once like. If you were not like that, then praise God for it. But I think that, if we are honest, there is a touch of every one of those things in your past and in mine. God took us when we were like that.

Let us look at five aspects of 3:4–7. Firstly, *What does it mean by "he saved us"?* Did I save myself? No. Did my church save me? No. Did someone else save me? No. Where did it all start? *It started because God is good and kind.* If God was not like that, I would never have been saved. If God was simply a just God and not a merciful God; if there was no kindness or goodness in him, just holiness, then I would never have been saved. But God is good and he has loving kindness—literally, the word here is "because God has philanthropy". The word "philanthropy" means to love people, and if you are philanthropic you put that love into action. God has done something about my need.

Secondly, we are told here of the *condition* of salvation. I want to underline 3:5. We have thought a lot in this letter about good deeds. But the danger is that I have left in your mind the impression that if you do good deeds you are a Christian. Here Paul instructs Titus to make it absolutely clear: he saved us not because of deeds done, not because of any merit of ours, but because of his mercy – not our merit but his mercy. That is the condition. I don't need to have done good deeds to be saved. Indeed, I am glad about that because if I had to do a lot of good deeds to be saved I don't think I ever would be. The Christian does good deeds not to try to get to heaven but because he is on the way there by the mercy of God. Never get the order wrong. How often people say, "But surely souls are good enough to go to heaven." As soon as they say that, they have clearly got it the wrong way around as if you are good enough first and then you get in on the grounds of that. If anybody gets to heaven it will not be because of a single good deed. It will be because of the mercy of God. But I would hope that, having received all the mercy and the salvation which the Lord offers, that is now expressed in good deeds – which is a very different thing. Ephesians 2 tells us that we are saved by grace *for* good works; we are not saved by good deeds, we are saved for good deeds. If you can grasp that, you have got the Christian gospel.

Thirdly, the *content* of salvation—what does it mean to be saved? It means both regeneration and renewal. The word "regeneration" means to start life all over again. Not just to have a new start in life but a new life to start with. For regeneration means new creation, something new has happened, and when I believed in Jesus and when you believed in Jesus as Saviour, God did a miracle in your heart. Every time that "old man" of yours comes up again you don't like the look of him because you look at him now through the eyes of your "new man" – your new life. Not only is the instantaneous miracle of regeneration given to you, but that crisis begins a process of renewal which quite literally means spring cleaning, a process of renovation. When we reach spring cleaning time we renovate a place – it is a process of making it clean, bright and attractive. So the crisis of regeneration leads to the process of renewal and a life is spring-cleaned by the Holy Spirit of God. There is to be a renewal of so much in our lives.

Fourthly, we think of the *carrier* of salvation—who brings it to us? We need to know this. Who is it who makes it possible? The answer is: God the Holy Spirit. God the Father loved us and planned it all. God the Son died and made it possible. God the Holy Spirit brought it into my life. I was born again of the Spirit. I am renewed in the Spirit – it is all in the Holy Spirit. Now Paul uses a phrase, which is rather important: *whom he poured out*. There can be no doubt what Paul is referring to here. It is exactly the same phrase as used of the day of Pentecost: "poured out". It refers to a Pentecostal experience of the Holy Spirit, which obviously happened to Titus and to Paul though they were not present on the day of Pentecost. It obviously happened to those Christians to whom this was written though they had not been there at the day of Pentecost: *which he poured out upon us richly*.

It is one thing to have had the Spirit touch your life, it is another thing to have had the Spirit poured out. He is an overwhelming experience. Read Acts 2 right through. The promise that was fulfilled on the day of Pentecost was this: "I will pour out of my Spirit upon all flesh." Later Peter says, "This which he has poured out you can see and hear."

Not only does Christ want to give us a new life to start with, he wants to pour out upon every believer of his Holy Spirit in such fullness that the believer is drenched in the Spirit of God richly. He is the carrier and he brings everything to us. Every single thing that Christ bought, the Holy Spirit carries into the believer's heart. Did Christ buy forgiveness? The Holy Spirit brings it to you. Did Christ buy liberty? The Holy Spirit will bring you into the liberty of the Spirit. Did Christ buy holiness for you? The Holy Spirit will bring it. Did Christ buy the resurrection of the body by his death? Then the Holy Spirit who raised him up from the dead will raise us up also.

Fifthly, the *consequence* – things happened as the result of our salvation. There are many other things that happened, but here are at least two. We were acquitted, justified. It means to stand in the dock and hear the judge say, "Case dismissed, innocent, acquitted" – to know that never again can you be tried on that charge, and the charge was the charge of having sinned against God. When you are justified you walk out of that court so excited, so thrilled, knowing that God will never again charge you with that.

Something in Roman law is interesting: a man who was condemned forfeited all rights of inheritance and was not allowed to inherit any legacy. So if he went out of the court justified, he was also pronounced the rightful heir of all that was due to him. That is why Paul goes on to say here: not only am I justified and acquitted but I am an heir of God.

I don't know if you've ever had a legacy left to you, but whether large or small it can be quite an unexpected and pleasant surprise, but I would rather be an heir of God, a joint heir with Christ, than inherit all the millions anybody could leave to me here. To be an heir of God, to know that one day you are going to inherit all God's property – talk about treasure in heaven! So we are heirs in hope of eternal life.

Verses 8–11 are concerned with practical matters and vv. 12–15 with very personal matters, and the letter finishes. There are three words in the practical section that pinpoint what Paul wants to say: *apply, avoid, admonish*. If you underline your Bible, underline the three words and you have got it. We are to apply ourselves to good deeds. That means to give thoughtful, diligent attention to doing good deeds. They don't happen automatically. A person may say, "I'd love to do good deeds and I feel I just want to do them," but that won't get them done. You need to apply yourself to it and to apply means to think what good deeds need to be done. Then you have applied yourself to thinking about them, and then you apply yourself to: "How can I do them?" – so you need to apply.

As against those who are going to do something about it, Paul in vv. 9–10 writes about those who prefer to talk rather than to act, and who prefer to spend endless time in discussing things rather than doing things, a temptation to all of us. So in v. 9 he writes, "Whereas good deeds are profitable and useful, useless, stupid controversy is unprofitable and futile." You can waste a lot of time discussing things that just do not matter. One of the favourite debates among the Jewish scribes was how many angels could stand on the head of a pin, and they could debate that for hours, literally. This scribe would get up and say this, and that scribe would get up and say that. What a stupid controversy! They would all have been far better off applying themselves to good deeds. There is a place for discussion, there is a place for study, there is a place for asking what is the truth. But if we waste our time on quarrels over the Lord, genealogies, dissensions, stupid controversies, then we are wasting our time.

In v. 10 Paul goes one stage deeper with more serious trouble. When you get such stupid discussions you get some people who have no other ambition but to divide, to form parties, one around themselves, and after you have told a man once or twice to stop doing this, if he does not listen then you must have nothing more to do with him. He is a dangerous man who, just for the sake of intellectual exercise, is splitting the fellowship.

Finally, there are some lovely personal touches. Paul wants to spend the winter with Titus so he is saying to him: I will come halfway to you if you will come halfway to me. I am in Macedonia; you are in Crete. Halfway between the two was a little seaside resort called Necropolis. Paul was telling Titus he would winter there. If Titus would try to go, Paul would send two replacements for him. He obviously wanted fellowship with this man. Then he said: "You've got two people that I have sent with you now, Zenas the lawyer and Apollos." Now "the lawyer" could either mean a Roman lawyer or a Jewish lawyer. Either way Apollos and Zenas had been sent to try to teach them the right attitude to the Lord. The thing to notice is that the church should see that Christian servants like this should lack nothing. Let us be quite practical about this. When somebody comes to help you, to teach, to preach, see that they lack nothing and let the people of the host church learn to apply themselves to good deeds.

All who are with me, send greetings; greet those who love

us in the faith. There are people who love us outside the faith and it is grand to have their love. You may have unbelieving relatives who love you outside the faith, and it is a good thing to have such human love. But I will tell you something more wonderful: those who love us in the faith. Somehow the relationship then is a double one. Not just for time but for eternity, not just because of a tie of flesh and blood, but because of a spiritual tie. Your real family are those who love you in the faith – they are the family you are going to spend eternity with. These are the people you should greet. Not just those who love you but those who love you in the faith. They are your brothers and sisters.

Finally, that lovely word comes in again, a word of which Paul never gets tired: the word "grace" – free gift, undeserved, unmerited favour of God – "Grace be with you all. Amen."

Read Philemon

A. PERSONAL TRANSFORMATION

1. Appealing advocate: Paul

2. Returning runaway: Onesimus (= Useful)

3. Offended owner: Philemon

B. SOCIAL REVOLUTION

1. Love
    a. Paul's child
    b. Philemon's brother

2. Law
    a. Public opinion
    b. Political opportunity

C. SPIRITUAL REDEMPTION

1. Sin
    a. Crime
    b. Punishment (atonement)

2. SALVATION
    a. Change of status (justification)
    b. Change of state (sanctification)

One of the most surprising things about the Bible is that no one intended to write it. It is a collection of songs, letters, poems, historical records. None of the writers, forty of them, writing in three languages over fourteen centuries, realised they were writing this book, and this is particularly true of the letters of the New Testament.

Perhaps the majority of the pages of the New Testament are simply letters that someone wrote to someone else. Most of them were written to churches, and therefore are rather formal and rather theological. But scattered among the pages of the New Testament are letters from one Christian to another. God has made a selection of these letters and has made clear: this is what I want in my Word; this letter is my truth; this is the medium through which my Spirit can teach people, right from now until the end of time itself.

So we have a little personal letter, which Paul hastily scribbled off to Philemon and sent by runner to the town where Philemon lived. Now why is it there? What has God got to say to us? What is this little letter doing in the pages of our Bible? I am going to approach this letter at three different levels to show you that you can go deeper and deeper into the Word of God and find more and more in it.

The first level is to ask what it tells me about the personal life of the people involved. Try to get into the letter. Try to see the people who wrote it, those who read it; the people who are mentioned in it, as real men and women of flesh and blood with temptations, passions and weaknesses just like me, just like you – to see how the grace of God can take very ordinary people and transform them and make them quite different. The devil would love you to believe that you can't change human nature, and this book gives the lie to that all the way through.

There are three people involved in this little letter: Paul the writer; then the reader, Philemon, and the man whom the whole letter is about, namely Onesimus, which is the Greek word for "useful". That is quite a name to have! It was a slave's name, so the name was given by his owner – no doubt in the hope, which proved false, that he was going to be a good servant. I am quite sure that no parents would saddle their child with a name like that for life. The situation is very simple: the slave had run away from his master. The one place that runaway slaves made for was the vast metropolis of Rome, to hide themselves there in the crowd. In Rome Paul was imprisoned, in chains. I don't know how a runaway slave hiding in the back streets of Rome found his way into the place where Paul was incarcerated, yet they met.

This little letter is simply written to the slave owner, saying, "I'm sending him back to you –" because when the slave met Paul, he discovered a Christian and he became a Christian. When Paul said, "Where do you come from?" he told him the story. When Paul said, "Who was your master?" the most amazing coincidence took place. Paul said, "I know your master, he is another Christian. Therefore there is only one thing to do: you have got to go back" – a very difficult thing to do. Paul gave him this covering letter to soften the reception he would get.

Let us look at Paul the writer, and realise that the man who wrote this letter is completely different from the man you first hear about, breathing threats and slaughter, and after the blood of Christians – to throw them in jail and to punish them. Here is a man pleading that a runaway slave be let off; a man who had been harsh and cruel when you first saw him, but now a man who is loving, kind, gentle and peaceful. What has happened to Paul? He has got older – but, sadly, age doesn't always soften a man. It should do, it mellows most things in life, but sometimes age makes people more difficult, more selfish, more harsh, more critical, so it can't just be age that has made the difference. Then again, Paul has suffered a great deal, and suffering can mellow people, but not all people. Some are hardened and made bitter and resentful by suffering, so it can't be that. We can see that Paul has changed.

Here is Paul, he has aged now, and would have been between fifty-five and sixty. Before you jump to conclusions, that was aged for those days. The average length of life then was twenty-six! Considering the privations he suffered, he was an elderly man. Not only is he elderly, he is imprisoned and chained to a Roman soldier with six feet of chain so he can't do anything in private. Is he depressed? No! Is he frustrated? No! Is he inactive? No! Nothing can bind a man of God. You may chain him, you may throw him into jail, but he is a man who will still go on doing the Lord's work.

Consider the notes that are sounded in this little letter. The first is the note of *gratitude*. An old man who is spending his remaining days in jail is thankful. Would you be?

The second note that is sounded here is *joy*. You must have sensed that as you read the passage. You got the sense of vivid joy that comes through this exuberant little letter and yet this old man is sitting in chains.

The third note is *confidence* – optimism, boldness. Get your guest room ready, I'm praying that I get out of this jail and come and see you, so you make up the spare bed! Here is an old man who has not given in.

The fourth note I find here is *humility*. He is saying: "I could demand this of you, but I don't – I ask you. I could say this is the right thing for you to do and tell you to do it, but I don't. I want you to do it because you want to." Here is a man who is not throwing his weight around any longer.

The contrast between the man who wrote this letter and the man who was stalking along the Damascus road some thirty years earlier is marked. What is the secret? The answer is that he has been a prisoner for those thirty years – a prisoner of the Lord Jesus Christ. He has been chained to Jesus for that time. The thing is that if you live with someone at close quarters you will inevitably become like them, you can't help that. Husband and wife become like each other. Their facial expressions begin to reflect each other. If you live with someone for thirty years, you will be influenced by them and particularly if they are a stronger character than you.

So the result was that Paul, having been chained to Jesus, a slave of the Lord Jesus, a prisoner of Christ for thirty years, has taken on Christ's character. Now I pity the Roman soldier who is chained to Paul. He is going to be deeply influenced, but fancy being chained to a missionary permanently! Can you imagine that? Again, the stronger character would influence the weaker. That is why Paul was able to win soldiers for Christ from Caesar's household during his imprisonment. Nor was he confined in his activity. First of all, he is a man who is *given to prayer and intercession*. You may chain a man up in jail but you can't stop him praying. Prayer is going to break out of that jail and change people. Paul, in this letter, says, "I'm praying for you. Whenever I pray for you I say, 'Thank you Lord for this man.'" So that is something you can do.

Sometimes elderly people say to me, "I can't do anything for the church now." They could do more than most of us who can get around – they really could. The trouble is that some of them have not developed a ministry of prayer so that old age finds them incapable of exercising this ministry; you can't suddenly pick it up. But I thank God for the elderly and confined people who can't get out of their little room but who pray and pray. God will one day reveal how much they have done for his church and for the world – and Paul, chained in jail, prays.

The second thing he does of course is *evangelism*. You can't stop a man of God having children. There is reproductive life in the man of God. So let us think this through a little further. Paul's message is: "Philemon, I have had a child in my old age, a boy that I want you to look after. His name: Onesimus."

I remember reading the book *Goodbye Mr. Chips*. As the dear old schoolmaster lies dying, he overhears some people talking about him. "Chips" is his nickname; his real name is "Chippings". They talk about old chips and one mentions the tragedy that he married and his wife died in childbirth and the baby died too, so early. The master is saying this to a junior who did not know of the tragedy. The junior says, "What a pity that such a man had no children." Chips lying on the bed hears this and he says, "What's that, what's that, no children? I've had thousands of them, and all boys." It is a lovely moment at the climax of the story.

Paul may not have been married, but he had loads of children. Onesimus, a runaway slave, was one of the last children he had in his old age. "My child...." This is how you feel towards a person you have led to Christ. You have become their spiritual father or mother in the sense that you helped bring them to birth. So this old man hasn't stopped doing this. I pray that when you get to your old age, you will not stop doing that. You can go on having children till the day you die in the Lord. Isn't that a lovely thought?

God had taken a harsh, cruel young man who was after people's blood and he changed him into this dear old man who is still having children in jail in his old age. Can God change human nature? Of course he can. Take the second person in this story, the main subject, Onesimus – a lazy, runaway thief, a slave who ran away from his owner, ran away with some money, and lost himself in the metropolis and his name was "Useful". Paul is now saying this man is really useful. You will find that he is a good worker, he wants to help; you will find that he is industrious, loyal and beloved. You won't be just getting a slave back, you will be getting far more than a slave; you will be getting someone back whom you will love, a beloved brother.

Now here is a very different person from the one we mentioned. Paul was an intellectual, a student, a go-getter. He was a leader and God took him and changed him. Onesimus – a poor little slave, probably born to slave parents, with no education and just trying to get out of work. Yet the same Lord Jesus took this man and made him a useful, beloved brother. It doesn't matter who it is, Jesus changes them.

The third person mentioned here is the reader, Philemon. Reading between the lines, you can get a picture of Philemon: he was a wealthy man of substance, a successful business man with a large house and many slaves – a man who should have been very self-centred, corrupted and possessed by his possessions; a man who could have been very typical of a lot of people in our world today in an affluent society. Yet what kind of a man has Jesus made Philemon? He is a man of love and generosity, whose kindness thrills people's hearts. Again, Jesus has been busy and changed this man. I don't care whether you are a slave, an intellectual, a businessman who has been successful – when Jesus gets hold of you, he will turn you into a person who is attractive and helpful and loving. Jesus is doing that every day, and this little letter is revealing these people who have been changed.

The result of all this is that every one of these three people was prepared to do something hard, something difficult, something that was against their nature to do. Let us look at

PHILEMON

what they had to do. First of all, for Paul, it was very hard to let his child go. Onesimus has helped him and comforted him, probably done his washing and brought bits of food to him in jail. It is a real wrench; Paul would love to keep him. But Paul, because he belongs to Jesus, says, "You must go back."

Secondly, it was harder still for Onesimus to go back. He could face severe punishment. He was going back into slavery, yet he went.

The third thing: it was very hard for Philemon to receive back a man who had been useless as a slave. Yet, because Jesus had touched all these people, they did the right thing even though it was difficult, and we have got this letter.

I would love to be able to ask some questions. Do you know that every page of the Bible raises as many questions as it answers? Just wait till I get to glory, I am going to just buzz around asking everybody what happened and "What was this, and what was that?" I want to know: did Philemon receive him? I want to know what happened. Could such an appeal to such a man fail? Did he do more, as Paul expected of him? Did he release Onesimus from slavery as he could have done and give him his freedom? What happened?

There is one tradition that is not in the Bible, it has come down to us through other sources of human tradition, that some twenty years later there was an elder of the church in the very town where Philemon lived, who was called "Onesimus". That is there in "secular" records. Did this slave become the bishop of the church? Did this slave become the elder, the pastor, of this group of people? Wouldn't that be a wonderful ending to the story if it is true? Well, I'll ask him when I get there.

But I would guess: if Paul's letter had failed and Philemon didn't have Onesimus back, do you think that page would be in our New Testament? Never! That letter would have been torn up and thrown in the waste paper basket. The very fact that it is there tells me that it worked and that Jesus brought these three men into his perfect will.

Now that is a personal way of looking at a little letter in the New Testament. Do we stop there? No, let us go deeper and ask what this has to say at a social level.

This letter is concerned with the greatest social evil of that day: slavery. Out of the millions of people in the Roman Empire, one of every three was a slave. Sixty million people were slaves, bought and sold like cattle or secondhand furniture in the marketplace, with no rights at all. Not even the right to life, for their master could kill them and it was not a crime. They had no right to family life, they had no right to property, they had no right to money. They were completely their owner's property.

Now of course, if that had applied today, and it still does in some countries, there would be protest movements, there would be armed rebellion, there would be guerrilla warfare, there would be terrorist uprising. How did Paul tackle this social evil? From this little letter we can learn of the Christian way to attack social injustice. There is a Christian way to do it, and if we don't use the Christian way we are in danger of establishing worse injustice.

At first sight, Paul seems to support slavery. He sends a man back into it. Paul did not lead a protest movement against slavery. Paul certainly did not talk about a revolution to overthrow the system, nor did any early Christian. Yet the letter to Philemon smashed slavery. How was it done? Paul has been criticised for sending Onesimus back. He has been criticised for putting in Ephesians and Colossians such words as: "Slaves, be obedient to your masters." Was he supporting the system? Are Christians committed to such injustice? No, let us look a little more closely. He did do something.

He loved the slave – that is the first thing. You cannot go

on ill-treating a person you love. Paul's love for Onesimus was the first thing that began to crack the situation. The second thing is that he appealed to Philemon to regard this man as a brother, beloved. That is the new wine which is ultimately going to burst the old bottle. To treat people with love is to treat them as people and not as things. The worst thing about slavery is that you are treating a person as an object, a piece of property, a tool. Paul injected into this system of slavery an attitude which regarded a slave as a person to be loved. That is the only thing that can ultimately cure man's inhumanity to man. Aristotle called slaves "living tools" because they had no rights and no relationships, but the Christian brotherhood abolished such language. Quite literally the earlier church was made up of slaves – that is where the early converts came from. They could only come to church with their master's permission, but there they were.

Yet they had been made free men and women in Christ; they had been made royal children, princes and princesses in God's sight. This gave them a dignity and a respect that nothing else could have given them. Paul said, "Slaves, be obedient to your masters" and he also said, "In Christ there is neither bond, nor free." No one is a slave in God's sight. Every Christian is a slave of Jesus Christ. This obliterates the distinction.

Centuries later, two things came about that enabled slavery to be banished in a major part of the world – two things that Paul didn't have. One: there was a political opportunity. That is necessary to improve social justice. In the Roman Empire, Paul didn't have political opportunity. Second: public opinion. Public opinion must so be influenced by this new thinking so that ultimately you can use public opinion to get rid of social injustice. It is no use protesting unless public opinion has been influenced by Christian thinking. It may be a slow job, but it is sure.

I remember going to Kingston upon Hull, and visiting a little museum by the docks of William Wilberforce's life and work, and seeing the horrible exhibits: the drawings of people packed like rats in the decks of ships crossing the Atlantic, so that at least a third of them would be dead and others would be diseased before they even arrived at the shores of the so called "New World". I saw the chains. I saw the horrible iron instruments used to torture slaves. I saw pictures of William Wilberforce, who said, "I will smash that" – and he did.

Do you know what one of his major weapons was in smashing it? The widespread distribution of the letter to Philemon, by Paul. But, you see, by this time, public opinion had been influenced by the Christian faith. There had been the evangelical revival of the eighteenth century. The last letter that John Wesley wrote before he died was to William Wilberforce, urging him to continue the fight so that out of the revival came social justice – and slavery was abolished.

I have in my possession, a letter personally signed by William Knibb, the Baptist leader in the West Indies, who described in that letter the midnight hour when the chains were broken up by the blacksmiths and men were free from slavery.

It was this little letter that inspired Wilberforce. It injected love into the situation and William had both the political opportunity and the public opinion to say, "Don't you see that these people are being treated like things"? Don't you love them? That smashed the injustice.

There is a great deal of social injustice in the world today. I used to go and meet slaves regularly in Arabia and talk to them. They were reasonably happy because they knew no better life. I would go into the Sheikh's Palace and go through the main area with its lovely swimming pool and everything else, into the back quarters, and there were the slaves. But in Arabia, there is neither political opportunity nor public opinion. Out of millions of Arabs, there are few Christians alive. Many have been killed. So it is no longer possible there to smash the injustice.

This is the way that Christians work: they get into a situation like leaven in the lump, like the salt of the earth, like the light of the world, and they inject love into the situation until people begin to see people as people. Then they smash the injustice by love. Here then is the second way in which we may look at this little letter and see it as a charter for Christian liberty and for the attitude to social injustice. What is needed is to love people as people, seeing them as those for whom Christ died. Can you go on ill-treating a person when you have that attitude in your heart? No. Receive him in a different way, Paul is saying to Philemon.

I am going to go even deeper into this little letter. Just one page, and we still have not plumbed its depths! Let me go now to the spiritual meaning. Let me see in the behaviour of these men the pattern of Christianity, *the pattern of Christ*. For the whole of the New Testament is based on this assumption: that the pattern of Christ's ministry to people is to be the pattern of our life toward each other. In this little letter I see a perfect picture of sin and salvation, because I see Christians reflecting the gospel in their lives.

First of all, I see here a perfect *picture of sin*. What is sin? It is to be a runaway slave. When God made me, he made me to give him everything I have got. He made me to serve him with my whole life. I am in the position of a runaway servant. He has not had from me what he should have had. Even at my very best, I am an unprofitable servant. I am like Onesimus, I am useless to God and I have run away and decided to live my own life and so I am just in this position. I am not only a runaway, but I have done what Onesimus has done – I have stolen my master's property. I have stolen the time that God gave me to use for him. I have stolen money he gave me to use for his purposes. I have stolen the gifts that he gave me to use – for me and for my benefit. I have stolen the very life he gave and said, "It's mine, I want it," and I have run away, tried to get lost. You see in Onesimus, a real live prodigal, don't you? You can see him on the run from his lord, which is precisely where I am in relationship to God.

Secondly, I see here, in reading between the lines and behind the lines, the punishment that is due for that. What do you think was the punishment for a runaway slave? The lightest punishment that a man would give if he was really merciful would be to brand the slave with the letter "F" on his forehead: *fugitivus*, runaway. And for ever afterwards the slave would bear that letter. Throughout the Roman Empire you would see men like that and you kept clear of them or you sent them back; you certainly didn't take them in. But the worst punishment, and the normal punishment, was death by crucifixion. If Paul had sent Onesimus back to a man who was not Christian, he would almost certainly have crucified him.

I have to tell you that that is God's punishment for runaway sinners: crucifixion. In other words, it is a crime deserving death. I can tell you, too, that in this little letter I see people behaving towards each other as God behaved towards me. First, Paul says, "I will pay all the debts. If he's robbed you of anything, if he owes you anything, I will pay. Here's my name, I sign it with my own hand." The New Testament takes up that too. If you were in debt in New Testament days it was made public. There was a sheet of parchment that would be nailed to a post in the middle of a marketplace, and your name and the figure would be up there.

I have read of a shop that decided to put its outstanding customers' debts outside the shop window, and there was quite an outcry. But it was common practice in the ancient world. If you had a friend who was prepared to pay your debt, he would go along to the marketplace, fold over the bond, as it was called, and he would drive a nail through it and sign his own name across it. Your debt was paid. In Colossians 2:14, Paul says, "Christ has taken the bond written against us and nailed it to the cross." Jesus has written his own name across my debts to God and said: "Paid. If he owes you anything Father, I'll pay."

There was no other good enough
to pay the price of sin,
He only could unlock the gate
of heaven and let us in.

In Paul saying to Philemon "I'll pay", I see someone behaving like Jesus. The atonement is there. Even more than that, Paul is prepared to plead with Philemon for forgiveness. He is saying: Forgive this man; he has run away from you, he is a bad lad, but forgive him. Not only do I have, in Jesus, someone to pay, I have someone to plead, someone to say on my behalf: "Father, forgive him."

Do you see the pattern? What God is to me, I must be toward others. What God was to Paul, Paul is toward others. So you have the flow of God's forgiving love going on into human society through ordinary lives. "Receive him as myself," says Paul. That is exactly what Jesus said to the Father about me. "Receive David Pawson as myself." Paul says to Philemon: welcome this man as if I was coming to you. Jesus says to the Father about everyone who believes in him, "Father, welcome them as if I were coming to you. Receive him for my name's sake." I see here a perfect picture of salvation.

Salvation is composed of justification and sanctification.

The first is a change of status and the second is a change of state. The change of status is: a slave into a son. When you and I came to Christ and were justified, the slave became a son. You are no longer a servant of God, you are a son of God, freely living within the family. Onesimus came back as a son, not as a slave – there is a change of status. The change of state is: *from being useless he became useful*. When I became a Christian I was justified and the slave became a son of God. The process of sanctification is to change me from being a useless creature to a useful man of God.

I finish with one lovely little phrase. Paul is saying something to Philemon: "Perhaps you could think of it this way – he ran away from you for a little while so that now he can be yours forever."

You might be on the run from God. Do you know what it is to run away from God? I do. I left home when I was sixteen. I wanted to get away and be myself and I wanted to go and work on a farm – and I left home and school as soon as I could and went away. All the upbringing I had, and the chapel-going lapsed because I got away from it all. I am so glad now that I did – it is worth getting away for a little while to come back for ever.

If we have been in the far country for a little while, we may appreciate the Father's house a bit more. You come back to it and find that all the happiness you went into the far country to seek was right at home all the time, where you should have been. I say to anyone who has come back to God: even though you have been away from him, think of it this way – you can come back to him forever, as a beloved son, as someone who can serve God, not because you have got to, but because you want to now.

Books by David Pawson available from www.davidpawsonbooks.com

A Commentary on the Gospel of Mark
A Commentary on the Gospel of John
A Commentary on Acts
A Commentary on Romans
A Commentary on Galatians
A Commentary on 1 & 2 Thessalonians
A Commentary on Hebrews
A Commentary on James
A Commentary on The Letters of John
A Commentary on Jude
A Commentary on the Book of Revelation
By God, I Will (The Biblical Covenants)
Angels
Christianity Explained
Come with me through Isaiah
Defending Christian Zionism
Explaining the Resurrection
Explaining the Second Coming
Explaining Water Baptism
Is John 3:16 the Gospel?
Israel in the New Testament
Jesus Baptises in One Holy Spirit
Jesus: The Seven Wonders of HIStory
Kingdoms in Conflict
Leadership is Male
Living in Hope
Not as Bad as the Truth (autobiography)
Once Saved, Always Saved?
Practising the Principles of Prayer
Remarriage is Adultery Unless....
Simon Peter: The Reed and the Rock
The Challenge of Islam to Christians
The Character of God
The God and the Gospel of Righteousness
The Lord's Prayer
The Maker's Instructions (Ten Commandments)
The Normal Christian Birth
The Road to Hell
Unlocking the Bible
What the Bible says about the Holy Spirit
When Jesus Returns
Where has the Body been for 2000 years?
Where is Jesus Now?
Why Does God Allow Natural Disasters?
Word and Spirit Together

*Unlocking the Bible is also available in DVD format
from www.davidpawson.com*

Lightning Source UK Ltd.
Milton Keynes UK
UKOW06f1152061015

259961UK00001B/4/P